M000078248

Parenting
with
Perspective

PARENTing

with

PeRspective

Kim Meyers

Foreword by Rev. Dr. Leanne Hadley

 invite
PRESS

Plano, Texas

Parenting with Perspective

This book is printed on acid-free, elemental chlorine-free paper.
ISBN 978-1-953495-18-1

21 22 23 24 25 26 27 28 29 30 – 10 9 8 7 6 5 4 3 2 1
MANUFACTURED in the UNITED STATES of AMERICA

Dedication

This book is dedicated to first and foremost my husband, Dan, who helps me be the best parent I can be.

Our son Cody, who made me a mother.

Our son Dylan, who completed our family.

I am so thankful for the people in our lives who continue to help us do life. These people are too numerous to list, but you know who you are.

Contents

Part Three | Let's Talk About How to Work Together

PARENTing

with

PERspective

FOREWORD

The day my youngest child walked across the stage during his high school graduation, I let out a huge breath of relief and felt my shoulders completely relax for the first time in over twenty years. Until this moment, I had not realized that parenting had been so stressful. This surprised me for many reasons. First, I had loved, and still do love, every moment of being a mom to my kids! Second, my kids, besides being sassy teens and driving too fast and too confidently in snowstorms, had been easy kids. They had done well in school, and we had a great relationship, so I had no huge reason to worry about them. Third, I was entirely unaware of the stress I was under. But when my son walked across the stage, I felt myself relax, and I realized that the stress I had felt was not because of anything my children did or did not do. It came from a deep place inside my soul in which I had secretly wondered everyday of their lives, "Am I a good mom? Am I doing this right? Am I messing my kids up?" This vein of self-doubt had rooted itself deep inside of me ever since I became a mother.

On the outside, I had been confident and getting along just fine. The stress I felt did not lead to depression, nor did it affect my day-to-day life, but when it left me on graduation day, I realized just how uptight my constant self-questioning and worry had made me.

Now, when a child graduates from high school, believe me, it is not the end of the parenting journey. Parenting is a life-long gift. But for me, in that moment of my son's milestone, I thought, "I guess I am pretty good at this parenting thing, because I have raised three kids, and they are doing just fine!" At that, I relaxed.

I share this story with you, because when I read this book, I kept thinking of how much I had needed a book just like this when my kids were younger! I did not need any more books about brain development, proper nutrition, or how to communicate better with my kids. I had all of those books already. I needed a book that named my fear of not being "enough" for this huge job of parenting and that reassured me that I could do it!

I hope this book will be as affirming for you as it was for me. Read it and accept the truth that is found in it. Parenting is complex. You will be unsure. You will not be a perfect parent every day, and your kids will not be perfect every day. But know that you are enough. God gave you this child. God is with you in your parenting. And no matter what happens in your parenting journey, you are not alone.

Reading this book reminded me that there are no perfect parents and no perfect children. There is, however, perfect love. The love you have for your child mirrors the love God has for you and for all of us. We are, while imperfect people, surrounded by the perfect love of God, and because of that, we can be the parents God has called us to be.

I pray that this book will be a companion for you to remind you that you are enough, that God is with you, helping you every step of the way, and that your child is blessed to have a mom or dad who loves them as much as you do!

Rev. Dr. Leanne Hadley

Preface

This book is not a how-to book about parenting. My bookshelf is already full of those resources. This book is a friend when you need one because parenting is hard. This book is about allowing yourself to trust your instincts and knowing when you need to seek guidance from others. This book is oozing with grace because we all get it wrong sometimes, but we need to keep going. Parenting is one of the hardest things I have ever done in my life. Parenthood brings me the highest of highs and the lowest of lows. It makes a mundane Tuesday a little more unique and a whole lot messier.

My parenting journey started with disappointment from lost pregnancies, fear while on hospital bed rest, and all before even having a child. I will never forget the drive home from the hospital. We prayed, cried, and worked toward being parents, and now we have a tiny human. At first, we were ecstatic. Then things became real. The dog eats the diapers. The child does not nurse. The amount of laundry is insane for something so small. But, in the moments of crazy, there are giggles, snuggles, and a love that I have not felt before.

This book will help you see that your family is unique and special. You have your own rhythm and quirks. You are different from your parents, your neighbors, and your friends.

This book is what you pick up when the moments are too much: the toddler tantrums have put you over the edge or the teenage angst is just too thick at the dinner table. This book will remind you of the love that is still present in those moments, that it might just be time to adjust your perspective, to know that the sun will rise tomorrow and that bedtime will come soon.

The book is divided into three parts:

1) Who you are as a parent. We must recognize who we are and our gifts, passions, and quirks to understand where we will need guidance and where we will soar as parents.
2) Who your child is. This is a difficult thing to do as a parent, to recognize who your child is and not who you envisioned them to be. This is constantly growing and changing.
3) How you can work together as a family unit. Parents, children, family, and friends are all going to be coming and going in your life. You need to be able to find a rhythm that works for your family, and you will.

The other intentional part of the book is that each section starts with scripture and ends with a prayer. Scripture is how I keep myself and my family focused on who we are in our core, children of God. Some days you might turn to a chapter and the Scripture may bring you the clarity you need. This was done with purpose and intentionality. Some days you might need to turn to the chapter about kids and read the prayer because that is just what your soul needs to pause and gain perspective. The prayers are written by my people, the people I just could not do life without; some are pastors, some are friends, some are family. I also asked different experts to add Parenting Perspectives in each chapter. This helps add dimension and diverse viewpoints to each section. I am deeply thankful for all the voices who helped make this book happen. I hope that this book brings you some joy, grace, peace, and ultimately some perspective.

Kim Meyers
Frisco, TX
May 2021

Parent's Prayer

God, as I navigate this journey of parenting, remind me that I am good enough. On days when I feel riddled in self-doubt and exhaustion, remind me that I am good enough.

Remind me that on the messiest days there is great joy in a paint-covered table, in a smelly tweenager who refuses deodorant, or in a moody child. Still there is great laughter to be found around the table or on a couch together.

Remind me that at the very core of everything I do, community matters most. Whom I surround myself with will teach my children whom they need in their lives too.

As I take a deep breath, bring peace to my heart, laughter to my soul, and love to each part of my day. Keep me grateful for the endless grace that is given to me on this adventure.

Bless the food on my floor, the dishes in the sink, and the decorations that have stayed up well beyond Halloween. Bless the little hands doing homework, the laughter on the playground, the mismatched clothes, and the newly independent drivers.

Remind me of the sacredness of parenthood and family—in all its many shapes and forms. May my children always know how loved they are.

Help me to remain their greatest cheerleader and greatest advocate. Amen.

As you read the pages of this book, I hope you feel seen, celebrated, and loved—just as you are.

Jennifer Ward Kloeppel
CEO of Showers For All, and a mama of 3

ParT one

Let's Talk About

You

1 You Are Good Enough

For we are what he has made us, created in Christ Jesus for good works, which God prepared beforehand to be our way of life.

Ephesians 2:10

The Perfect Parent Does Not Exist

When my kids were young, I bought a coffee mug (one of my shopping weaknesses) that said "World's OKest Mom." I loved this mug. It made me laugh, but it also resonated with what I considered to be realistic expectations of myself as a parent. I will volunteer, but I probably won't be "homeroom mom." I will listen with a soft ear, but I may scream sometimes. I love Jesus, but I don't always have the patience of Job. I will make your lunch, but I may substitute a Lunchable at least one time a week. I would be an "OK" parent. When my six-year-old saw that mug, he was angry. He would not accept "OKest" as a description of his mom. I had to put the mug away until he became a teenager when the mug became funny (and some days true).

I tell you this story because when it comes to parenting, perspective is everything. There are days when you think you have it all together and end up leaving your high school freshman standing outside the field house waiting for a ride to play in his football game, as you are busy inside the field house and forgot he needed a ride.

Some days, you will think you are the worst parent ever, and then in a moment, your child will remind you of something you said that made the day better. Reminding yourself that you are good enough will be necessary. You need to believe this to get through each day.

How you define parenting will help determine the expectations you have of yourself as a parent, how your children see you, and most of all, how you see yourself. I hope you realize how amazing and special you are as a parent and that no one can be a better parent to your children than you. Parenting is not an easily defined set of guidelines you can follow in order to create a "perfect" home, but parenting is a path you forge. Each parent's path is unique, special, and personally crafted. Parenting is an adventure in relationship-making. Your parenting style is molded and influenced by hundreds of different sources. In being a parent, you bring with you your childhood, your partners' childhood (even if you are a single parent), the social media perfect parent and the social media hot-mess parent, your child's specific personality, and the many factors that have influenced and continue to influence all of those mentioned above. The idea of a "standard" perfect parent does not exist. The "perfect" parent for your children is you. No one is perfect, but the fact that you are trying means that you want to be the best version of yourself for your family. That means that you are already good enough.

You have the skills to be a parent. Some of them will come easy to you, some you will need to work on. But you can do this. Some days you will have it all together, and parenting will be the best thing that has ever happened to you. Some days you will want to hide in your closet so your kids can't find you. But you are good enough. You may not be the best parent. You are surely not the worst parent. But you can choose to learn and grow. Continue to remind yourself that you can do this.

Stop comparing yourself to others. You are you. Your parenting style is different from your parents, your neighbors, and the blogger that you follow. As you read, take what you can, make it your own, and keep on going. Books are one dimensional and black and white. But your parenting life is full of color. I always try to remind myself that humans have been parents for a long, long time. Even Jesus' parents lost him for a few days.

When you think about your parenting, know who you are. Understand your gifts, understand your weaknesses, and live into them. I know that I tend to overreact to situations. I respond strongly, and then when I gain perspective, I find myself in a sticky situation because of my initial response. I know I need to pause. I need to give myself some time before I respond as a parent. I have a husband who is much calmer when it comes to quick reactions. When we lean into each other's gifts, we typically have the best outcome. This did not happen overnight as parents. Understanding our personalities is something that we learned as the days, weeks, and years kept moving. We learned about and from each other.

We tend to put a lot of pressure on ourselves because parenting is a big deal. We are helping a soul live into whom God has created him or her to be. Yes, that is a big deal. But, if we go through each day worried about our decisions, overthinking our reactions, and not leaning into our strengths, stress will consume us. Parenting will eat us alive. Repeat this mantra each and every day: "I am good enough. I can do this."

Trust Your Gut

One of the million things that makes parenting hard is that so much of it is a gut reaction. I don't mean that deep thought, knowledge, and research are not essential in the parenting journey. They are. But when your gut tells you something to trust, you need to go with it.

Our culture has an expression that says, "when people show you who they are, believe them." This expression is the same when it comes to parenting. We will do the research, ask our friends, do a poll on our Instagram stories mainly to confirm or deny our gut. I am a learner. It is in my nature. I love to read, and I love to research things. I love to process decisions out loud with anyone who will listen. When it comes to parenting, I do the research, and I ask my friends. I talk about parenting issues for hours with my husband. Ninety-nine percent of the time, I come to the same conclusion as my gut reaction. I craved confirmation.

A simple rule is that any decision made from intense emotion is typically not a good one. So, you need to give it some time. I am telling you to trust your gut, not run around always reacting to it. Listen, lean in, learn, and use your gut as a parenting tool. We have many different expressions for our gut. God's voice in our lives, the power of the Holy Spirit, instinct, clairvoyance, feeling, foresight, or even hunch. No certain one of those makes for a sound parenting practice alone, but combined with prayer, research, and processing, that is parenting at its best.

We nearly always start with our gut. Often, when people say "trust your gut," we mean trust the decisions that are easy to make:

- This daycare does not feel right for our family or child.
- That friend may not be the best influence in our child's life. (Good luck with this as they get older.)

Some gut instincts tell us that we as parents must watch and wait, keeping a safety net waiting for our children when they fall.

I believe fully that my gut reveals the power of the Holy Spirit living in my life. The Holy Spirit is the nudging voice that I feel leading me in the right direction. This feeling does not end when you become a parent but becomes even more robust (and tricky to discern) because of the love you feel for your children.

I love many things in this world: sushi, a nice cup of coffee or glass of wine depending on the time of day. But I don't have a passion or a deep, profound love for any of these things compared to my family's love. This deep love for our children and family, while beautiful and wonderful, can, however, make gut decision–making super hard. It can make us want to fix things for our children or can make us react to our gut instead of trusting it. Take a deep breath and use all the gifts God has given you to make wise decisions. Trust your gut. Then temper that trust with your gifts of discernment and knowledge. But above all, trust that you are your child's advocate and that you ultimately know best. Then breathe again, check your emotions, say a little prayer, and do your parenting thing.

5-5-5 Rule

This rule is simple, yet it helps me time and time again. It has helped my five-year-old and fifteen-year-old alike. So, put it on a sticky note and place it on your bathroom mirror.

When something happens in your life or in your child's life that feels awful or dramatic, ask yourself, "What will this feel like in 5 days?" The answer is that it probably will still have a sting. What about in 5 weeks? Ninety percent of the time, the situation will begin fading into a memory. In 5 years? Most of the time, this will be something you have grown from and put into long-term memory.

Let's look at it by example.

Elementary School

It is 9:00 a.m., and you get a phone call from the school. A 9:00 a.m. call from the school is typically not a good thing. They sometimes call for awards, but not typically at 9:00 a.m. You wonder if it is the school nurse, the teacher, or the principal before saying hello.

"Hello?"

"Yes, is this Mrs. Meyers? I am Principal Smith. I need to talk to you about your son. He isn't hurt, but he did _____."

- cut a classmate's hair.
- stole from the prize box.
- talked back to his teacher.
- pushed a classmate, caused an injury.
- stole from the café.
- lied to the teacher about _____.

OK, now is the time to pause. Take a deep breath, because each of the items listed above brings various emotions to a parent, depending on your personality. Here is what happens if I am receiving this call: I start with anger. How in the world could he do something like this? Then I would begin judging myself. What kind of parent am I? Then I would be embarrassed that my child did such a thing.

Now it is time to listen to whatever situation happened at school. Respond with, "We will talk to our child about this when he gets home. Thank you for calling me." Hang up. It is essential to recognize that in the moment of the phone call, the situation feels tremendous. At this moment, we must put some perspective on our parenting.

Now, ask yourself: Will this be a big deal in 5 days? 5 weeks? 5 years? In elementary school, the answer is typically no to all three. This is a lesson you and your child can learn and grow from.

Middle School

You are now in the fun stage of parenting where you no longer plan playdates. Your child is finding some pockets of independence, and you pray a lot more about your child's decisions, the ones he or she will make independently from your guidance.

Let's play out the 5-5-5 rule when it is not a discipline problem but a decision that has consequences. (Don't they all?)

Your child comes home from school after hanging out at the park with friends. He looks pale and nervous. You keep a watchful eye, and your gut tells you that something significant happened today. You keep going about your day, waiting for your child to reveal what is bothering him. Depending on his or her personality, it can happen quickly. Or not. Some children will hold onto anything that might disappoint a parent until they burst. Our family rule is please just tell us before another adult does. We don't like to be surprised.

Your child eventually says he needs to talk to you. At the park today, he played basketball with friends and put his school-issued band instrument on the side of the court. After the game, when he went to get it, it was gone.

OK, this is a big deal, but my son is safe. He did not harm others. In oversized deal items, I'll take it. Apply the 5-5-5 rule. In 5 days will this be a problem? 5 weeks? 5 years?

The lesson learned will help your child take responsibility for mistakes. It is essential to remind yourself that this is not your problem. This is your child's problem. You can guide him or her with solutions but you must allow them to solve them. In the case of my son, the consequences are clear.

- He needs to talk to the band director.
- He needs to figure out how to work to earn money to replace the instrument.
- He will never leave the instrument unattended at the park again.

See how this helps put things into perspective?

High School

I love teenagers. This can be something that people think odd about my personality, but the life of a teenager is full of emotions, growth, change, and it is a powerful and transformable time in your child's life. This is a time in parenting where you begin to see how they are growing into their gifts. You get to see how they fix their problems and seek your advice (at times). This is also the time where kids lean into their friendships for advice and mentoring. You begin to have to let go in ways you know are healthy but can still sting. In our house this is the time when dating started. Teen emotions can feel profound. So, let's use the 5-5-5 rule with a teenage breakup.

Your child comes downstairs with tears on her face about her breakup. Each child will react differently to stress or trouble, but ice cream and loud music seem to work with my children.

When she is in a place to listen, ask her if in 5 days, she will feel this strongly about the breakup? In 5 weeks? In 5 years?

The most important part of the 5-5-5 rule applied to teens is to wait until they are in a place to listen. In the height of emotion, listening to advice on putting a feeling into perspective typically will not go over very well. But, when they are calm, help them learn how to see what this decision will look like over time. Gaining perspective is a life skill that you will want them to have.

The 5-5-5 rule helps me as a parent, a leader, and a friend. It is a multifaceted rule. I believe that this rule works because it allows us to pause and put situations into perspective. It allows love and grace to seep into the problem. It enables us to breathe in the breath that connects us back to God.

The Bible verse that opened this chapter is Ephesians 2:10: "For we are what he has made us, created in Christ Jesus for good works, which God prepared beforehand to be our way of life."

In this passage, the author reminds the people of God that we are created for good. We are created in the image of God, not to be God but to be children of God, created for good. Parenting is hard, but it is also good. You are good. You are good enough!

Parenting Perspective: Tara Tevis
Parent, Counselor

I can remember when I was in my final semester of graduate school. I was preparing to lead a small filial therapy group with three to four parents participating. In the group, I would be teaching them some of the basics of play therapy so they could have a "play session" with their own child, a therapy that can really help a child to feel understood and accepted by their own parents. It's a great way to strengthen a bond between parent and child that may have become fragmented. I was terrified that the parents I was working with would have no faith in me. I was so afraid they would ask me, "Have you done this with your children?" And I didn't have children. I was young, newly married, and still working on my education. I had no experience or perspective as a parent. Why should they trust that I could be of any help to them? Although I knew I had a good education (almost a master's degree in counseling) and good training through my program, there was so much I didn't know about being a parent!

Well, fast forward twenty years. I now am a mother of two, and I'm not sure I am any wiser about what guidance I could offer a new parent struggling with their child. I have learned that there is no magic formula, theory, strategy, or technique that always works. All kids are different and respond differently. But simply deciding to become a parent makes you ready for the job. You signed up. If you are invested in raising a human being with the intent of doing the best you can, then you are qualified for the job. You will do some things well and some things not so well, but you've got this. And as it turned out, none of the parents I was working with in my graduate program questioned my ability to help. They were willing to trust me. They were so thankful for the guidance. I was the only one who had a lack of faith in myself. I didn't yet know that I could do it.

I have always held on to an idea that was presented to me by Dr. Garry Landreth, an expert in play therapy. I think this is one of the most liberating and useful concepts that I have used with my own children.

The basic idea is that it doesn't matter what you have said or done. What matters is what you say or do after what you have said or done. As a parent, you will mess up. You will lose your cool or make a bad decision or say words to your child you would never dream would come out of your mouth. It happens. But you can always make it better. You can go to them and say, "I made a mistake. I am sorry. I should have handled this differently."

I think this is so important for so many reasons. First, this gives all parents the permission not to be perfect. You are not expected to have the knowledge and ability to handle each challenging situation with your child perfectly. There. Done. You don't always have to get it right. Second, you can accept and admit when you have made a mistake. You are modeling for a child how to accept personal responsibility for your actions and demonstrate remorse. It is not always easy to admit when you are wrong, especially if you are really hot about something! However, it is a very powerful (and in my opinion, critical) moral lesson that we need to model for our children: accept responsibility for when you have made a mistake, and then apologize or try to make amends. It's not about dwelling on the fact that you blew up at your toddler or that you screamed and scared your five-year-old or that you forgot to pick up your middle schooler. It's about what you do after that. This is the piece they will remember and grow from.

You won't always get it right, and that is OK. You

aren't supposed to always get it right. But you can re-flect on what you did or what you said and have a con-versation with your child about it. You can explain that you were upset, emotional, and didn't handle things in a good way. You can promise to try to do better next time. Kids are very forgiving. Thank God for that.

Oh Holy God; Love, Giver of Life, Redeemer,

*I need you. Make me aware of your presence . . . always . . .
even right now.*

*Remind me when I forget,
"My grace is sufficient for you."*

*When I lose my temper
"My grace is sufficient for you."*

*When I fail today
"My grace is sufficient for you."*

*When I compare myself to others
"My grace is sufficient for you."*

*When I feel like I am not enough
"My grace is sufficient for you."*

*When I think I am right
"My grace is sufficient for you."*

*When I am critical
"My grace is sufficient for you."*

*When I don't take time to listen, to laugh, to be intentional
"My grace is sufficient for you."*

*When I don't have it all together
"My grace is sufficient for you."*

*"My grace is sufficient for you."
And because of that, I am enough. Remind me of that today.*

*Whisper your love and grace to me so that I can speak
and show it to others.*

In your most holy and precious name, Jesus Christ, I pray. Amen.

Rev. Sarah Marsalis-Luginbill

2

You Can Learn and Grow With Your Children

Brothers and sisters, I do not consider myself yet to have taken hold of it. But one thing I do: Forgetting what is behind and straining toward what is ahead.

Philippians 3:13 NIV

You Do You

Let me state for the record that both my husband and I have great parents. We were raised in great homes and with parents who loved us thoroughly and allowed us to make mistakes. We did not grow up in perfect homes because perfect homes do not exist. Even though we grew up in great families, we have parenting styles and personalities different from our parents. We are not our parents. We have our own personalities, gifts, and weaknesses.

Have you ever had that moment where something flies out of your mouth, and you sound just like your mother or father? At times in my parenting journey, this moment gives me a pause and a smile. At other times, I stop in my tracks and think: I have become my parent . . . eek!!!!

The truth is I have not become my parent. But they significantly influenced my life, so they still speak into my life as a parent.

I am not able to speak into the life of people who grew up in a home that was not full of love. But I can speak into wanting to be myself when it comes to parenting. I want to learn the good and bad and create a pattern that works best for my family.

Now let's recognize where you came from and where you are going. I have always been a weird combination of a peacemaker and a troublemaker. I strive to be a parent who allows my children to learn and grow in powerful ways. My personality, the peacemaker, doesn't easily allow my children to make mistakes, feel pain, or experience uncomfortable situations. But I know who I want to be as a parent. So, I have had to set up expectations for my children (and for me) on "saves." For example, if they forget their lunch, need football equipment, or need school supplies, I am happy to help, under these expectations:

1) I will help if I can, but I might be in a meeting or busy working on something.
2) You get one save a semester. Is this your one?

These expectations help me say no sometimes, which has never been an easy thing for me to do. It also allows my children to think through if they rant, need help, or figure it out. About 90 percent of the time, they figure it out. This is a parenting win. So, let's go back to why I ultimately set up this rule. On the outside, it looks like I am setting up good problem-solving skills for my children and concrete expectations for our relationship. We all know the real reason is that I love to save my kids. It makes me happy. It brings me joy. But it is not where I want to go as a parent.

When I am working with couples who are about to get married, I have them list three to four things that they want to bring into their marriage from their family of origin and three to four things that they don't want to bring into the marriage. This practice can also be completed with parenting. Let's give it a try.

Ask yourself (and your partner):

- What are three to four parenting skills from your family of origin that you want to bring into your family?
- What are three to four parenting skills from your family of origin that you do not want to bring into your family?

If you have a spouse or co-parent, compare lists. Talk about it. Notice what will come naturally when it comes to parenting and what will be a struggle. Plan for that together, to be a team when it comes to being your best self and best parent.

Know To Whom You Are Speaking

As we learn and grow with our children, it is important to recognize their stages. This helps with our children's expectations and allows us to know how their brains are working now.

I have to say that brain development, learning, and faith stages are something that I can totally geek out on. How the brain works is 100 percent fascinating to me. I will try my best not to geek out on you, but just know this section gives me the warm fuzzies.

You can put parenting into four simple stages:

1) Early Childhood
2) Elementary
3) Preteen
4) Teen

We all know there is nothing simple about any of these stages; we also know they look a lot more like this messy infographic:

Early Childhood

    Baby

    Hungry baby

    Teething baby

    Crying baby

    Moving baby

    Talking baby

    Walking baby

    Falling baby

    Potty training

    Potty training . . . not working . . . do that again later

    Potty training II

    Toddler tantrums

Toddler FULL OUT CRAZY tantrums
Sweet, cuddly toddler
Picky eater
Throwing food on the floor for fun

Elementary

Getting dressed
Staying in bed all night
Losing teeth
Blowing their own nose
Wiping their own parts
Getting their own snacks
Packing a backpack for school
Homework
Social skills with friends, siblings
Using tone of voice to share feelings

Preteen

Hormones are starting; emotions are real and fast
Friend groups change, and that can hurt
Seeking independence from parents
Wanting all the help from parents
Study skills are growing
Interests are developing

Teen

Kind teenager
Angry teenager
Talkative teenager
Silent teenager
Learning to drive
Independent
Needs all the help all the time

Knowing something about each stage is important. You need to know whom you are talking to, what they can understand, and how they most likely will respond. We all know that individual children grow and learn and their own pace, but there are some overarching things that we need to know.

For example, kids don't begin to think abstractly until about age twelve. Here is an example that you can put in our bad parent column. When the boys were about eight and six, we had to put our two Labrador retrievers to sleep. The dogs had health issues. It was time. We told the boys one night, and it went something like this: "We have some sad news. Daisy and Diva are sick and old, and when we took them to the vet, we decided that they were not going to get better, so we and the vet decided to put them to sleep. They are now in heaven with Great Gram and playing with Jesus." We never told them that the dogs were dead. This is important for many reasons, but here is the rest of the story. About two weeks after, at dinner one night, our youngest said, "So, when are Daisy and Diva waking up and coming home?"

Dan looked and me, and I looked at Dan. We were giving each other the parent stare that says, "Say something; fix this!" Finally, one of us said, "The dogs are not coming home. They are now dead and in heaven." The boys cried. They cried a lot! It was a horrible night, but I now understood why they did not cry two weeks earlier. They thought the vet was giving them a chance to rest up and come home. This is a parenting product, where you forget that you are talking to a child who does not think or have the life experiences the way you do as an adult. They needed facts, the concrete facts, so that they could process them accordingly. We tried to make it softer, kinder, but in doing that, they did not process what happened. I could get on my soapbox on how to talk to your kids about grief, but suffice it to say, this principle applies to many topics. Did you know that a toddler can only process one emotion at a time? You can see this at a birthday party where they are having so much fun, and then their ice cream cone drops on the floor. They go from total joy to real sadness. Then you give them another ice cream cone, and their pleasure comes rushing back.

Ages and stages are also essential to know when it comes to faith development. If you are interested in finding out more about stages of faith there are several books available, including a well-known book by James W. Fowler, (James W. Fowler, *Stages of Faith: The Psychology of Human Development and the Quest for Meaning* (San Francisco: HarperSanFrancisco, 1981). Scott Peck also spoke about stages of faith (M. Scott Peck, *The Different Drum: Community Making and Peace* (New York: Simon and Schuster, 1987). The Scott Peck book is out of print, so you'd need to borrow it from your library.

I find charts and information like this handy for a couple of reasons:

1) You know where you are.
2) You know what can come next.

I am a person who is always looking toward the future, what is next in this adventure of life. When you see where you are, you can also see where you are going. This helps in so many ways when it comes to parenting.

When you are frustrated with the stage of life you are in, you can know that you will go to the next stage in time. This always helped me move forward with my kids. Some stages are so much fun that you just don't want to let them go. Some are so hard that you try to run through them. But each stage is essential and valuable. I might not have loved each stage at the moment, but overall, I could find joy in it. I have loved watching my kids grow into who they are, who they are called to be. It can be hard letting them go as they get older, but it is also awesome to have a changing relationship with your children. I can honestly say that most days, I love this teenage mom thing. It is hard, but overall, it is super cool to grow with them and see that they are becoming such independent and strong young men.

Notice the Moments of Joy

Seeing the world through the eyes of your children is one of the best reasons to have children. I genuinely believe that. When our youngest was about five months old, his brother would walk in the room and do a silly dance, and the giggles that would come out of this child made my day. I have a huge smile just writing about it.

I was a public school teacher for nine years before I went into ministry. I taught first grade for some of that time, and I loved it! Kids learn so much in first grade. They learn to read, like really read. They learn math concepts, the science of how things work. They master tying shoes. They start losing teeth (not my favorite part). They learn to understand social dynamics, and so much more! It was such a joy to experience these moments again and again with my classes. We have this same opportunity as parents.

Parenting is hard, but when we can change our perspective and see the joy in moments that could drain the life out of us, it helps us all be just that much better.

This is Why Toddlers Are the Best Thing in the World
Have you ever seen a toddler jump in puddles, find a roly-po-

ly, see a fire truck or trash truck? They find such joy in the little things. These are the same humans who throw themselves on the store floor when you tell them they can't have the $200 toy that dances with voice commands. They feel deeply. They need to know that we love them entirely, in their joy and their tantrums.

This is Why New Readers Make the World a Better Place
Learning to read is a slow process that starts when you hold your baby and talk to him or her. Learning the letters, the sounds, putting the sounds together to make words, and the words together to create stories is a lot of fun. When a reader begins, it is painful, but the moment it clicks, he or she can put together sounds and words to form a whole new world. This is why I loved teaching. This moment was one of my favorite moments in the world. We adults take for granted that we can read. Notice the joy, read twenty books when they get home, celebrate this new skill that will forever change them.

This is Why Gaining Independence Is So Powerful
The words "No Mama, me do it!" are some of the most frustrating English words a parent can hear. They typically come when you are already ten minutes late to school or a family gathering. You know that allowing your toddler time to click their own car seat will take an average of two minutes a click compared to the twenty seconds it would take you. But you smile and know that the two to four minutes will be worth it as they grow more independent. An old memory showed up on my phone, a time when our now fourteen-year-old would not take a nap. "I am now listening to my son scream, 'No happy nappy!'" The day that memory showed up on my phone was the same day that child set his alarm to wake up on his own,

started his laundry, and made his own breakfast, all while watching videos on his phone and not even looking up.

The steps toward independence are slow and painful, but they are worth it in the long run. As a parent, you will be able to help them move into their first apartment, knowing they can do it without you.

This is Why Teenagers Are So Fun

I can say with all honesty that I love raising teenagers. Seeing them transform into young adults is wonderful. One year our family went on vacation to Colorado. We signed up for a white water rafting trip, and because our boys were older, we were able to make a full day trip that had class 4 rapids. It was the first time we got to do "adult" things with our children, and it was so much fun!

The teen years are hard for parents because your children are growing away from you in so many ways. But when you look at it, they are supposed to do this, to be strong independent humans. They still call, they still ask for help, they still come and watch TV. Your child still has you, and they know it. They might even ask for advice (even though at this stage, parents know zero). Have fun with your teenagers. Know that you are still the biggest influencer in their lives, even if it does not feel like it.

Parenting Perspective: Vicky Dearing
Mother, Grandmother, Retired School Administrator

Brothers and sisters, I do not consider myself yet to have taken hold of it. But one thing I do: Forgetting what is behind and straining toward what is ahead.

Philippians 3:13 NIV

As a Christian woman, wife, mother, friend, educator, and professional coach, I've learned that it is best not to linger too long in the past, especially if the past brings sorrows, disappointments, hurts, and regrets. Rather, we can realign the life that we want by living in the present, holding onto our faith, and moving toward the future we desire. It's not that we ignore what happened in the past that may have harmed or disappointed us but rather that we look for what we have learned that will serve us and others as we move forward, as we "strain toward what is ahead." Most important, as we realign, we hold on to what is at the center of our being. We hold on to Christ and know that we are never alone. We are loved, even when at times we feel unlovable.

Parenting is not a smooth journey. There are times of joyous exuberance, pure pleasure, a sense of pride, and feelings of great and small accomplishments. There are other times when we feel exhausted, disappointed, hurt, and downright angry. Having different feelings is natural. Let's not ignore our feelings, suppress them, or sweep them "under a rug," as some of us were taught to do as children. Instead, let's recognize our feelings, identify what brought them on, and determine if those feelings are the ones that we want to hold on to or release as we move through the ups and downs of parenthood and life in general. This helps us keep our eyes on our bigger vision—one day standing face-to-face with Christ and hearing Him say, "Well done, good and faithful servant" (Matthew 25:21).

If you and I were sitting together, reading this book and thinking about the ups and downs of parenting, here are three questions for us to ponder:

1) What guides you as you move through the highs and lows of being a parent?
2) Because we know that God is love, what is the message that God is giving to you in the midst of your ups and downs of parenthood?
3) Since each day is a new day, how are you modeling for your children and yourself, ways in which you monitor and adjust your own emotions and behaviors when they are not in alignment with your desired vision of who you are at your core?

Remember that when you look up the word *strain,* you will find that it means "to make a strong effort." That, brothers and sisters, is a day-by-day process. Thank God that you are not journeying alone.

Loving God,

*I turn to you for the wisdom I need in any moment
as a parent. What takes me by surprise does not take you
by surprise. When things do not go as I've planned or anticipated,
help me embrace the situation as an adventure, see it as
my children see it, and allow it to teach me something new. Open
my eyes to their world perspective. May I learn with them.
For each stage of life, remind me of what it is like to be their age, full
of its unique struggles and growing pains. Draw me close to
your heart and grant me the ability to lean into my God-given
strengths and parent them according to this stage of life.*

*Lord God, you have given us minds to think and the creative power
of imagination to grow as your children. May I not take these gifts
for granted.*

*Thank you for entrusting these precious lives to my care.
In Jesus Christ's name I pray, amen.*

Rev. Sandy Heard

3   You Will Mess Up

I hereby command you: Be strong and courageous; do not be frightened or dismayed, for the LORD your God is with you wherever you go.

Joshua 1:9

The Way You Respond Counts

I would guess that the majority of parents who are holding a newborn baby have been told, "Enjoy this. It goes by so fast." After that kind stranger (who gives advice even when nobody asks) walks away, that sweet baby starts crying, has a massive blowout, and then spits up all over you. Moments like these feel big and endless. I get that. I have lived that. But yet the quote is true. As I am writing this sentence, I have a seventeen-year-old son and a fourteen-year-old son. They both are taller than I am, speak in deep voices, and are independent. Yet, I remember like it was yesterday when they were two, spilling a cup of milk on our kitchen floor, and crying about it for what felt like hours. That huge response felt silly to me as an adult. I had to realize that this feeling was real and big for a two-year old. OK, so I just became that woman at the park telling you to enjoy it. Sometimes, we do have unenjoyable moments. But I do want to let you know that when you mess up, it is going to be OK:

- The first time you lose your cool and scream at your children.
- When they go to school without a lunch.

- When you forget to sign the permission slip.
- When you forget to pick them up from school.

In the course of parenting, inevitably, something will happen. Mistakes will be made. You get to choose how you respond. I typically have two responses: self-loathing or self-judging and tears. Now, that is not always my healthy self, but it is my go-to reaction. So, I must know that about myself, learn to take a breath through the mistake, and move past it. I want to be clear here that mistakes in parenting will happen. This section is not speaking about abuse or mistreatment of children, which is different from making a mistake, but common parenting mistakes that we all make. We live in a world where social media defines our vision of life, and so people typically only put the good stuff out there. This results in a kind of illusion. We parents begin to tell ourselves a story that everyone has it together, except for us. This simply is not true. We are all human, which means we will all make mistakes.

When we brought home our first child, we had our moms come and stay with us for the first week. I will never forget one night when my sweet little baby would not stop crying. I was rocking him, burping him, and feeding him. At one point, I am pretty sure we were both crying. My mother-in-law came into the room and said, "Let me give it a try." I handed over the baby, who would not stop crying for me, and in minutes, he was calm in her arms. I then went to my own bed and cried into my pillow, sad that I couldn't even make my own baby calm down. The next day, I started with the wrong attitude. I felt little and weak. I was not. I was tired and overwhelmed.

Seventeen years later, as I relive that story, I can understand that my own anxiety and fear did not help calm my baby.

I don't remember how I turned my feeling of failure around, but I did. I would assume I did it with the support of my family and some rest. The cute baby helped.

Confession time: I once put my baby into a shopping cart, and the sections for the legs were broken. My baby tumbled to the floor. I caught him halfway, but he got a scrape on his leg from the broken cart. He was screaming, and I thought, "What kind of mother puts her baby in a broken shopping cart?" But then we both had a minute, and everything was OK.

Yet another time, my husband and I were driving to see friends, and I thought that my husband had buckled in our baby. He thought I had. We turned around to see him falling out of the car seat. This was easily fixable; we pulled over and properly secured him, and then drove on. But the feeling of "how could I do that," that feeling that the worst could have happened, stayed with me.

Then, there was that time when my third grader snapped at me with attitude, and I yelled at him. He went to his room and slammed the door. I ran to my room and slammed the door too. Not my best moment.

Then there was that time when I forgot to pick up my son from school (AGAIN).

Or, that time when . . .

Or, that time when . . .

Or, that time when . . .

Here is the point. You will mess up. When it happens, you can respond in a healthy and helpful way, or you can respond in an unhealthy and destructive way. Choose the healthy and helpful way. It will make you and your children better.

Mistakes Can Be Opportunities To Grow and Learn

This chapter is not about our children's mistakes but the ones that we will make as parents. Parenting is hard because our children don't come with a manual, and there is tons of information on how to be a good parent. It can be overwhelming.

There are some simple guidelines to parenting. Give them food, give them water, give them shelter, and give them love. I also add that faith development is a vital part of parenting. But these simple guidelines are just the tip of the iceberg regarding what it takes to parent well and raise vibrant children.

The little mistakes that we make as parents can feel so big. Sometimes what we call a mistake may simply be a judgment from other parents who might do something in a different way. But we all pretty much know when we have truly messed up. We yelled when we should have listened. We let them break a rule that we just did not have the energy to enforce. We did not make them finish dinner or eat their veggies. But along with each mistake comes the opportunity for grace and forgiveness. The grace that we give our children should also be given to us. Grace doesn't mean allowing ourselves off the hook. But it is allowing us not to hang on the hook. Grace is recognizing where we are and knowing where we want to go.

Take the example of the dinner table:

Your child does not want to eat the meal that you gave him. He likes chicken nuggets and only chicken nuggets with ketchup, but the ketchup cannot touch the chicken nugget. (We have all been at this dinner table). You have had one of those days where you are counting down the minutes until bath time and bedtime, and you just don't have the energy to make him eat dinner. You give up, and let him reject dinner.

Grace Option One: It feels good for a few minutes to have peace and quiet. But about five minutes later, you know that this will not work out well for your family in the long run. You stop, sit next to your toddler, and say, "Today at dinner, you did not eat the food I prepared for you. This means that tonight you can't have dessert."

You then step away from the toddler who is now crying again. You did what you could.

Grace Option Two: It feels good for a few minutes to have peace and quiet. But about 5 minutes, later you know that this will not work out well for your family in the long run. But tonight, you just needed the peace. You did what you could.

You need to do what works for you and your family.

Let's play out what it can look like with a teenager in the house:

You ask your teen to unload the dishwasher, fold towels, or clean the bathroom. She heaves a sigh, rolls her eyes, and walks away, still not completing the chore. You have had a long, hard day and don't have much more to give to your family tonight, especially patience. The second heavy sigh puts you over the edge as a parent, and you go into the five-minute lecture, screaming about how lucky she is and that she does understand how good she has it. You then take away the phone and ground her for a week. You both then storm off to your rooms, angry.

Grace Option One: You have a guilty cry in your bedroom and know you went too far. You calm down and go knock on your child's door. You say that you were frustrated with how she responded. You are vulnerable and honest and tell her that you had a hard day and overreacted. You tell her that she can have the phone back and will remove the grounding after she completes the chore.

Grace Option Two: You go to your room, and you get more worked up about how your child does not help around the house. You phone a friend (spouse, good friend, mom) and talk it through. You knock on your child's door and let her know that you were disappointed by her response but that you also overreacted. You will give the phone back, but she is still grounded because of the way she spoke to you.

You can probably think of about ten more grace options for each situation, but the primary steps are the same:

1) Breathe and gain perspective.
2) Admit where you messed up.
3) Say you are sorry.
4) Move on.

Each step is hard, but grace must be abundant in your life. I know I need it in mine. Grace helps me learn, helps me grow, and helps me gain new perspectives so that tomorrow can be a brand-new day.

Perspective is a Choice

Perspective is a great de-stressor in parenting. In fact, it is an absolutely vital de-stressor when it comes to almost anything in life.

The Merriam-Webster Dictionary defines perspective as

"a: a mental view or prospect" or "b: a visible scene, *especially:* one giving a distinctive impression of distance: VISTA." (Merriam-Webster, s.v. "perspective," https://www.merriam-webster.com/dictionary/perspective). I have noticed when I can gain perspective in a situation, it helps so very much. This is from the little upsets in life to the massive-deal situations. Putting situations into perspective in parenting can not only save you from self-blaming or self-doubting, but can help you to distinguish between the little upsets of life and those massive situations that require more serious intervention.

Let me tell you a story about our older son. One Saturday night, when he was eight years old, he went to bed as usual following all his regular bedtime routines. About forty-five minutes later, we heard crying. When we asked him what was wrong, he said he didn't feel right. After taking his temperature and seeing no impending illness, we calmed him down and put him back to bed. This time, he went promptly to sleep.

When I got to my computer, I found that my son had left me a note. Here is what it said: "I am 8 for the last day :-(, Oct. 20, 2012, last day of even 1-digit numbers. :-(bye 8."

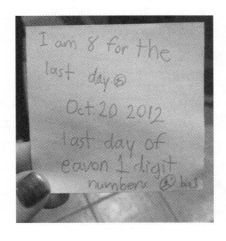

At first, I wanted to respond to his note, saying: "Really, kid?" But instead, it got me thinking. Wow, perspective really does make a difference. My son went to bed mourning the end of year eight. I would have gone to bed excited about the birthday of year nine. What if my boy had gone to bed excited about being nine? Perspective is everything.

Our kids learn most from what they see in us, the way we handle situations, issues, and life. I hope that my kids learn from me that life will be what they choose it to be. Perspective is a choice. We can be sad about what has passed, or we can focus on the future. When it comes to parenting, taking a moment in each situation to gain perspective has helped me through each parenting stage. Events and issues can feel huge at times, but putting things into perspective or looking at them from a different perspective can help us both see the bigger picture and be the best version of ourselves in any parenting situation. Perspective can make us more confident and more resilient. More confident and resilient parents mean more confident and resilient children.

Parenting Perspective: Sharon Rankin
Mother, Grandmother, Retired School Administrator, Kim's Mom

While living life over the last seven decades, I have come to a conclusion: my humanity shows on a regular basis. That can be good but can also be not so good. For example, several years ago I thought I was sending an email to a friend whose name began with the same three letters as our senior pastor. As my email program was giving me possible email addresses I could select from, I clicked on a name and email address. Yes, I bet you know where I am going. I clicked on our senior pastor instead of my friend. In a short period of time, I got an email from our senior pastor that went something like this: "Did you mean to send me this email or should it have gone to someone else?" I was so grateful that the email did not include a "bad" joke or some other such stuff. It was an email about church work but wasn't intended to go to the senior pastor. I quickly responded to him that I was sorry for the error and used my line that I use when I have made a mistake: "My humanity is showing again!" He stopped me the next Sunday to say that was a great way of looking at life and told me that would "preach." He used it several times in his sermons and said that he hoped it helped someone to see that humanity means that we will make mistakes. How we handle those mistakes is much more important. I found that this way of approaching "learning opportunities" worked with my staff while I was an administrator in the public school system too.

My humanity has been known to show when dealing with our family as well. Sometimes my "not so nice" side shows, and my humanity is definitely on display. After years of practice, I have learned that it is best to acknowledge my humanity, to own the mistake, take a breath, count to ten, and then do the only right thing: apologize for remarks or actions made and hope I will be given grace. It is not easy for me to admit my errors, but it sure is important for my soul and the person or persons I have offended.

My career as a middle school teacher and administrator provided many opportunities when humanity was on display. From the perspective of the adult in the room, finding ways to help students make better choices was the theme of my career. It is a given that we will all have times when we just flat mess up! As a middle school student, some of those choices made at school could be much worse if made as an adult. When working with parents and students, I tried to make it clear that what happened was a choice made by the student. Helping the student learn from that choice in a relatively safe environment could be a good thing. Some of the things that happen in schools include drugs, theft, and physical conflicts to name a few. As an adult, those choices could change someone's life in a very negative manner. My goal was to help parents and students see that learning from choices, being accountable for choices, and then being able to apologize for choices would build a better person in the long run. Was it fun to have these conversations when emotions were running high? No, not at all! Often, I would tell students never to forget that day when a valuable lesson was learned in a safe environment where staff and parents were there to hold them accountable with love.

Another of my attempts at helping students was to tell them to "keep your own power." What did I mean by that? When you make good choices you usually keep your own power and no one is there to tell you what will happen to you because you handed your power to someone else. I pray there are students out there that still hear those words in their head when tempted to make a choice that is not best for them. Will we mess up? We sure will. Can we learn from these opportunities? We sure can...both as children and adults.

When dealing with students at the middle school level, it seemed important that they learn to deal with the negative choices they made and then be ready to apologize for those choices. Forcing someone to apologize on the spot often is a shallow "sorry." After some divine intervention (I don't believe this was just my own idea), I came up with a three-step plan to help students learn the "art" of an apology. It has also worked for our grandsons and others who have crossed my path.

Step 1) After thinking about what happened, I am
          sorry for _____ (be specific).
Step 2) In the future I know a better choice would be
          _____ (be specific).
Step 3) Will you accept my apology?

Did this always work? Of course not, but it often did work. The students had a choice to write an apology that would be delivered in person or by me, or they could privately ask to meet with a teacher or staff member to apologize in person. I was pleasantly surprised how many students chose to do the apology in person. We also talked about the fact that an apology is useless if they don't change their behavior and learn from the opportunity. Will they mess up again? Probably so, but they now have some skills to help them practice "owning their choices" and moving forward.

As a teacher, I found I also had to learn to be "corrected" by my students. There are several choices on how to handle that situation. Our humanity seems to want to give us a reason for our mistakes. We like to think our mistake was probably someone else's fault, as we are "perfect." Over the course of my career, I learned that turning mistakes into "teachable moments" was a much better way to go. When I misspelled a word on the board, I usually thanked the student for being so observant. I would then ask them to look it up in the dictionary and make the correction on the board (now you would suggest they use their digital device to find it)! That worked so much better than going on the defensive that I had had a bad morning or showing anger for their lack of respect for the teacher. While coaching teachers, that is a strategy that is always included in ways to turn the not-so-good moment into a teachable moment.

So, will we mess up? Of course we will. It is how we handle that "mess up" that is important. When humanity strikes again, hopefully we can own it, deal with it, and then try our best to turn it into a learning opportunity personally and as a model for those who are involved in the mess up.

When we pray The Lord's Prayer, we are reminded, "forgive us our trespasses as we forgive those who trespass against us and lead us not into temptation."

Jesus gave us this as a way to deal with times when we mess up, because we will mess up. But hopefully, we will learn from it.

Lord, meet me in this mess.

My life feels likes my house when I can't invite people over for dinner because things are a wreck and I don't want you to see it.
BUT
I need you to see it.
I need you to see me.

I know you are here with me, at the top of this unsteady pile of broken promises, angry responses, manipulated mistakes, and regrets. I know you see it all and you love me ever still.

Remind me that grace is your lifeline of redemptive hope and the only strength I need to walk down from atop this pile to see the table already set.

At the table we can only be fed if the bread is broken . . . if brokenness is shared.

Lead me to sit. To be still. To receive. To be filled up.

And when I rise from the table and the mess is still all around me, may I be satisfied, sustained, and secure in knowing it is all gonna be OK because, come what may, you and I are in this together.

Thank you, Jesus!

Rev. Ashley Anne Sipe

4 You Need to Take Care of Yourself

So then, a Sabbath rest still remains for the people of God; for those who enter God's rest also cease from their labors as God did from his. Let us therefore make every effort to enter that rest, so that no one may fall through such disobedience as theirs.

Hebrews 4:9-11

Learn to Say No

Everyone says it. You must take care of yourself to be able to take care of others. The best illustration of this is the oxygen mask on an airplane. They tell you to place the mask on yourself before you put it on others. I have always wondered how this works. Does it play out in real life? Do parents follow this direction? I understand the why behind this, but how do we do this?

This is what I can tell you: I have been a parent for seventeen years. I have had times of excellent self-care and times when it was nonexistent. I know for a fact that when I take time outside of my family to take care of myself, my whole family is better for it.

When I take the time for me, I can feel guilty and somewhat selfish. But good parenting requires good self-care. For every parent, time out must be nonnegotiable. I've developed various self-care rhythms that have worked for me throughout my parenting journey. Here are some of my favorites:

- Gym time
- Walking/jogging

- My counselor
- Bubble baths
- A shower
- Getting my nails done
- Bible study / Connections with God
- Hair appointments
- Girl's Night Out
- Date Night
- Saying no to something
- Laughter
- A day in bed watching Netflix
- Cleaning/organizing
- Being at home alone
- Family time / Easy Movie Night / Game Night

This is not a final list. But they all reflect my attempts at self-care at one stage or another.

I remember when our older son was about two months old. A lovely shower felt like an adequate self-care regimen. This is not sufficient self-care anymore. A shower is just a part of my day, and I no longer include that in self-care. When it comes to self-care, you need to recognize where you are and where you want to be.

When my children were babies, I needed time just to be me. This was when long walks or girl time was necessary. Now that my children are older, a nice laid-back family night fills my soul just fine. I have always been a better mom when I get to sleep, drink my water, eat healthy meals, and move my body. This is not rocket science. We all know this. And yet we find reasons why other things matter more.

Let's take a moment to recognize the power of saying no

as self-care. I have finally found the joy in a well thought out no. This can be volunteering, a work assignment, or even a night out. There was a season of my life in which I said yes to everything, because I did not want to miss anything. The FOMO (Fear of Missing Out) has always been real in my life. I have always wanted to be part of the group, the club, the party. So, when people asked me to help, it made me feel seen, and in that quick moment, the yes felt pretty good. Then, the yeses piled up, and I found myself doing things to help my kids' school, my church, and my friends, but I had little time left for my own family. That was not my intention or my plan.

I now always respond to an ask with "let me think about this." At times, I ask a coworker before I say yes. Other times, I talk it over with my husband. Sometimes, a simple pause allows me to recognize my reason for saying no.

A Step-by-Step Process of Self-Care

The process of self-care as a parent is not easy. It can make us feel selfish. We can imagine that we have zero time for it. The truth is we can't afford not to do it. We must first take care of ourselves so that we can be healthy to take care of others. Find a self-care routine that fits what you need. For example, if you need rest, self-care can look like you are setting a time to go to bed and going to bed at that prescribed time. Maybe for you, it is a nap. Perhaps it is a night alone at a hotel. You must figure out for yourself what you need and what will work best for you. The only self-care that works is the self-care that you can and will do. Your needs will change as your life changes around you.

Here is the starter kit for self-care: notice that you need it. This can honestly be the most challenging part of self-care.

It would be best for us as parents if we could always take good care of ourselves, but we will inevitably have times when we are great at it, and times when we aren't. We will have better luck in following through with regular self-care if we set apart specific times that we can spend doing the things that nourish and feed us. Setting up solid self-care practices during these times is essential. Sometimes this means setting up a network or community of people who can step in so that we can step out. Having people around who can help us succeed in life and in parenting is vitally important.

Our needs can change through the various stages of our lives, and at various times, our need for time out may feel greater than others. But we will feel more nourished if we are keeping a schedule of "reboots" we can look forward to so that we know a needed break is coming. Depending on what stage of parenting we find ourselves in, we may need to adjust the kinds of breaks we need to feel refreshed and reenergized. Here are some examples of self-care in each parenting stage:

Infant

If you are in a marriage, set up one day where one parent is "off." The off-duty parent gets to sleep in and do things for himself or herself.

If you are single, find a friend or relative who needs some baby snuggles. You can give yourself two to four hours of break time by dropping your child off at their home. This time is all yours. You can sleep, run, eat, dance naked, whatever you might need during that time.

Toddler

When my children became toddlers, birthday parties started taking over our lives, and some days the last thing in the world

I wanted to do was go to a bounce house and make small talk. So, I would tap out and let my husband go without me. Sometimes, I would do the same for him.

I would get my nails done, go for a jog, or sit on the couch and read a book.

Sometimes, I would spend that time catching up on things I didn't have the time to do during normal family or work hours. This lowered my stress level, because it made my schedule easier to handle.

My husband loves being outside, and his happy place is fishing. When you take a toddler fishing, it is no longer restful or relaxing. Finding time for him to get away and just have some quiet time outside was key.

Younger Elementary

In elementary school, sports began to take over our lives. But every sport does not need to become a family affair. You don't need to drag all of the siblings and both parents to every practice and game.

If I did go along to the practice, sometimes I would go for a walk around the field to take time for myself. If I didn't go along, I could take time for myself in other ways.

Some of you might love to cook. It may be your form of self-care. I am not in that category. I cook because my family needs to eat, simple as that. During these years, the Crock-Pot became my dear friend so that when we got home from work, dinner was practically made. For me, doing this left me time to do things I truly enjoyed.

Upper Elementary

I found that some of my best self-care during the upper elementary years resulted from teaching the kids to take care of themselves. Teaching them to pack their lunches, do their laundry, and clean the house freed up time for me. These were life skills that would teach them how to take care of themselves, while giving me the freedom of no longer packing daily lunches.

These upper elementary years can be a big rhythm change for the family. As your family is growing and changing so are your needs as a parent. Pay attention to what works for you, what your marriage needs, what you need to recharge and be the healthiest person you can be. Due to the busyness of this particular phase, some friends of mine found that just some quiet time reading a book, going for a run, or just being alone is exactly what they needed. Yet, some of my other friends were the exact opposite, they needed to recharge around other people and in a group. The key to self-care is just that—do what works for you.

Middle School

Middle school is the stage of parenting where I started going back to see my counselor. Middle school is when you begin letting go as a parent. It's a time of emotional change not just for your child but for you too. A good counselor or therapist can be that extra support system you need to navigate this new time when your kids change and your parenting role changes.

Middle school is hard as a parent. Your children are changing physically and mentally. This is also the time when they can begin to pull away from family and connect with friends in a deeper way. I know many parents who choose this time to seek counseling for themselves. As your children are changing and growing, this time with another listening ear, a trained listening ear, is vital in helping you be the best parent you can be. This perspective from outside of your home speaking into your life can really be helpful. This can become a safe room to talk through work, friends, family, and marriage.

Middle school kids can have a crazy schedule: band, football, baseball, church, friends, and the list goes on. What can you do as a parent to take a break from the crazy? To have time alone, or time together? What do you need? Make sure to ask that question and then put it on a calendar and make it happen.

High School

In high school, family night became the most cherished part of my self-care. The boys were now hanging out with friends, working, and studying. Some substantial family time was right for my soul. Family time could be a night of golf, a family movie night, or a trip to the zoo, time when we got to laugh together and reconnect as a family unit.

The other important piece for me was date nights with my spouse. OK, I realize that this is important in all parenting stages. But in this stage, we felt the clock ticking toward the empty nest. It was essential to know we started this together (without the kids) and that it was our goal to end this together.

College and Adult Parenting

The first thing that comes to mind when parenting a college or adult child is the need to stay connected but not take on the responsibility of being in the driver's seat for their decisions. Be a support for your college or adult child but remain clear on what decisions are theirs to make and what are your own. In this stage, boundaries are essential.

Self-care in this parenting stage often simply means letting go of the part that is not yours to hold onto. Your children will fail and fall, and you can be there to help pick them up, but you can't fix their problems. Your role is not always to keep them from falling but to be sure they know there is a lifeline to help them get back up. Letting go of control also means letting go of worry, stress, guilt, and unnecessary responsibility. You have raised them thus far. Now it's time to let them make their own mistakes and learn from them, as they go on to raise their own children.

Apart from the boundaries, the best self-care you can practice at this point in your parenting journey pertains to finding things for yourself to do, to rediscover your own interests, hobbies, goals, and identity as a parent of an adult child. When your whole world has been wrapped up in your children for years on end, when they grow older, it can feel like a part of you is gone. Find things to round out the parts of you that you have not had time to nourish. Consider what feeds your soul as you enjoy the time to focus on yourself instead of devoting so much time and energy to others.

Spirituality and Self-Care

I am a Christian parent. I know that saying this sentence can conjure up many different images, phrases, and emotions. This is what being a Christian parent means for me: simply that I am not alone in this journey; God is woven into all that we are and do. I want to recognize that, to honor that, to strive to love others fully. I believe that raising my children with Christian beliefs does not make me or my children "better than" others. I believe that connecting to God can help your family in so many ways (and I get into some more details in chapter 9), but this section is for you as a parent. How can connecting with God on a daily basis help you? When you stop even for five minutes, take some deep breaths, listen to the world around you. This is connecting to something greater than yourself.

As parents we are so very busy. At some stages in our lives a shower is a luxury; in other stages sleep can be the golden ticket of the day. In this business we get very "intra-centric." We only think about what is happening in our daily lives, the lives of our family, the short term. When we stop to connect with God, we can regain some perspective. As parents we have so many responsibilities, and it can be overwhelming to balance them all. God helps me balance.

This connection also allows me to see my children (and all people) as children of God. This especially helps when my children are being rather difficult. I can breathe and remember that God loves them fully when I have moments of fault when it comes to parenting. As I read scripture, I am also reminded that God calls imperfect humans into leadership. Again and again God uses our gifts and talents to make this world a better place. This gives me hope for my journey.

I grew up in a Christian home. I am now an ordained pastor in the church. I don't know how to do life another way. God centers me. God helps me see the greater perspective. It is like when you are typing on a computer and you can pick left, right, or center justification. When I read a devotion, say a prayer in the morning, ask God where I can be a light in the world, cry to God that today is hard, sit in silence with God because I have no words . . . all of these things help me hit center. My faith and my connection with God put me on the path each morning to be reminded that I am called to love others and that I am not alone in this journey. I can't imagine doing life any other way.

Parenting Perspective:
Rev. Ugonna Ooka Onuoha
Parent, Pastor, Hospital Chaplain

So then a Sabbath rest still remains for the people of God; for those who enter God's rest also cease from their labors as God did from his. Let us therefore make every effort to enter that rest, so that no one may fall through such disobedience as theirs.

Hebrews 4:9-11

You Need to Take Care of Yourself

Sabbath, from the Hebrew term *Shabbat* means "to rest" or "cessation." This term goes back to the creation story in Genesis where the Creator rested on the seventh day of creation. The Christian tradition takes this story and creates the seventh day as a day of worship and rest. While we are created in the image of the Divine, we are also created with the need to rest.

In the book of Hebrews, the phrase "Sabbath rest" signifies a promise of arduous work ceasing and culminating in a weekly holy day, not simply a day of inactivity. Sabbath is a set-apart time for reset, joy, and renewal. It echoes the practice God began in the story of the Ten Commandments in the book of Exodus. God created the heavens and earth in a work schedule for six days and then rested on the seventh. God commands us humans to do the same—to follow the example God gave for us.

Sabbath as God prescribed when practiced thoroughly is how one cares for self. It is also both critical and essential.

The Value and Curse of Self-Care

Self-care is "a multidimensional, multifaceted process of purposeful engagement in strategies that promote healthy functioning and enhance well-being." (K. E. Dorociak, P. A. Rupert, F. B. Bryant, and E. Zahniser, "Development of a Self-Care Assessment for Psychologists," *Journal of Counseling Psychology* 64, no. 3 (2017): 325–34.) Self-care is vital for building resilience for those stressors in life that you cannot eliminate. When you take care of your mind and body, you are more fully equipping yourself to manage and live with stress.

Self-care includes the individual practices of health management apart from the aid of a medical professional. In health care, self-care is any human regulatory function that is under individual control, deliberate and self-initiated for the purpose of the maintenance of health and well-being.

Taking care of yourself so that you meet your own needs allows you to better support people you care about. When you take care of yourself and are less stressed, you are better able to take care of the needs of others.

There are a multitude of ways to practice self-care:

- Go for a brisk walk; journal; play games
- Engage your senses in art, crafts, or music
- Take a bath; get a massage or facial
- Schedule social time
- Deep condition your hair

- Deep clean your pores
- Nourish your skin
- Get a manicure or pedicure
- Consume healthy diets with meals right for your body
- Get regular exercise
- Get enough sleep
- Meditate; get counseling
- Care for your soul; forgive; read; sing; worship

How do we do all of the above or just some of them? How do we care for ourselves? It must be different for everyone. One person may care for themselves by going for a jog while another person would feel torture doing so. One person may like to read or write, and another would just feel frustrated by this. Start by asking yourself when you feel the most joy and peace? How can you tap into that joy? How can you find a peaceful moment in your day? What does joy look like? What does peace look like? Create a ritual around the joy—create a moment around the peace. If sitting outside in the sunshine brings you joy, take a mat outside and a stick of incense and create a moment for yourself. If you find joy and peace in the kitchen preparing dinner, clear everyone out, pour yourself a cup of tea or a glass of wine, turn on the music you love, prepare dinner, and flourish. If you enjoy your daily cup of coffee, light a candle before you pour your cup. It is the simple things that slow us down, make us pay attention, and allow us to tend to our spirits. These small moments can be momentary Sabbaths.

There are also larger Sabbaths—days of worship and days of solitude and rest. Regularly our bodies tell us that we need rest, that our bodies and minds need to step away sometimes to sleep, meditate, be alone, read, zone out, and ponder the world. Rarely do we listen (especially as parents and busy people). Finding a balance in our lives between the work we do and the rest we need is difficult. When the demands of a job call us, when the job we have is a job we love, when our work is never done, it seems that rest is the last thing we think about. Our culture tells these lies, untruths, and we have been trained to "just do it" rather than "just be it." The challenge comes in stopping the mental loops we have before our bodies stop us. If we can get a grip on the mental strain that stress perpetuates, then stress cannot have its way with our bodies. You have heard of people running out of steam or burning out. This breaking point happens because we do not hear the call to rest before it becomes cataclysmic. Rest whispers to us and challenges us to listen before it must scream.

Rest is one of those things that we must start before we think we need to start. When you first roll your eyes or feel flustered, start there. Listen to what your mind and body are telling you at that point and take a moment. There are certain roles in our lives that we cannot put aside—being a parent, a sibling, a child, a caregiver, a partner/spouse—until roles change with a loss or separation. There is one role that will never change—that is the role of self-caregiver. If a person does not choose that role, they will not survive well. Choosing self-care is not selfish, it is self-preserving. It is taking care of the gift given to us, taking care of the one life we have; preserving the one spirit we have within us is essential.

None of this is easy because as a parent and caregiver, there are expectations that people have of you. One important key is to consider that you will do a better job filling that role if you can take time for yourself. It is OK to tell people that.

In those larger moments of Sabbath rest, make sure to let people know you are taking time for yourself and that you will not answer your phone. Turn your phone off and take time to sit in the state of being a self. Do what feels natural for you and also what nurtures you—clean, sleep, dance, sit, lounge, cook, journal—whatever provides the nourishment and rest you need.

Tell your children that you are taking care of yourself and this will help them learn the value of self-care. Tell your partner or spouse that you need recovery or downtime and this may encourage them to take time for themselves. Expressing this need for self-care can also keep you accountable.

Rest is a blessing; the curse is that we need it. Our bodies, minds, and spirits need rest to continue to be a blessing to the world and to take that time for those who are closest to us.

Let's Talk About Mental Health

Mental health is defined as a person's condition concerning their psychological and emotional well-being. Mental health addresses how one attends to one's ability to cope with the normal stresses of life. How a person works productively and contributes to the community with ease. The World Health Organization explains that mental health is a positive state of mind and body, feeling safe and able to cope, with a sense of connection to people, communities, and the wider environment. One can also look at mental health by exploring the seven dimensions of wellness, which include physical, intellectual, environmental, vocational, social, emotional, and spiritual health. Research shows that a balance among these seven dimensions leads to a fuller, more satisfying life.

Physical health focuses on practicing healthy daily habits that enable one to feel well in their body, to move more, and to eat well. These elements are vital to building strength, flexibility, and endurance and to helping prevent diseases to add quality years to one's life. Experts encourage a complete wellness approach, which certainly includes good self-care. It is important to integrate exercise, nutritious foods, personal safety, and moderation of alcohol consumption. When it comes to exercise, everyone is different. Support whatever fitness goals and levels you develop for yourself. You may feel at home in a workout group while others find a place to enjoy the solitude of a quiet run, a yoga class, or stretching. One must make time and commit regularly to an activity that interests them.

Intellectual health includes self-care activities that boost one's brain. An active and open mind leads to a life filled with passion and purpose. Energize your brain with an enjoyable book, a thought-provoking class, or a seminar. One can further engage and apply this dimension of well-being by engaging in creative activities, games that help to keep the mind sharp. An example of this may be a crossword puzzle or card game that makes you think.

Environmental health has as its goal to love the earth. In doing this, we help the planet, and it brings a sense of accomplishment to our own life. Our daily habits can affect the health of the ecosystem and bring positive effects to the world around us. Try composting, buying organic foods, or using clean products for your home. Use less plastics. Reuse items. Recycle.

Vocational health calls us to live a life with a purpose. This well-being category of self-care focuses on enriching our life and that of others by sharing unique gifts, skills, and talents. Whether through work or volunteering, one can make a positive impact and reap the health benefits of adding purpose to one's life.

In social health, we connect with others. When we nurture relationships with family and friends, we create healthy support networks for life. Personal connections contribute to a long and fulfilling life. As with COVID and other grim times, one can continue to nurture this dimension through digital and virtual gatherings by Zoom and other platforms.

The practice of gratitude enhances our emotional health. Expressing love helps us achieve balance in the face of challenges. Self-esteem and optimism are powerful healers. Being mindful and living in the moment are powerful antidotes to anxiety and depression. They bring happy tomorrows and make life worthwhile. Start a journal and list three things you are grateful for each day.

Spiritual health asks us to nourish our soul. One's set of beliefs or values can shape how one lives one's life and will also help to create harmony. When we are willing to look for meaning and purpose in our life, we will find inner peace, rest, and joy, which are the goal of good self-care.

Developing a Personal Self-Care Plan

- Know that self-care is not a one-size-fits-all strategy. Customize your own self-care plan to meet your needs. For example, self-care for a busy college student who feels mentally stimulated and has a bustling social life might include the need to emphasize physical self-care. On the other hand, a retired person may need to incorporate more social self-care into their schedule to meet their social needs.
- You might access which areas of your life need attention and self-care. You might reassess your life in the event your situation changes physically and financially; your self-care needs will require adjusting to address the change.

- You do not have to tackle everything all at once. It is essential to find one small step or area and begin caring for yourself in this area.

A Personal Self-Care Journey

Self-care is an expression of faith and trust in God who invites us to rest; it is also essential to a life of discipleship in a world where so many things do not make sense. In my work as a hospital chaplain and spiritual caregiver to patients, families, and staff, I have witnessed many joys, tragedies, and grief in my work.

The pivotal moment of ultimate commitment to practice what I preach about self-care came after the death of my twenty-three-year-old daughter, Agnes, who died in March of 2019. Agnes had been ill since before she was nine years old with a painful and chronic autoimmune disease. Agnes struggled with her pain, and our family watched with an inability to take away her pain. In the days following Agnes's death, I remember returning to work and having to care for other families who were experiencing the illness of their child. I felt unable to accompany them because of a shared grief that hit too close to home.

As I began to yield my brokenness to God, I had to believe that life is worth living and then to create a path for it. Although it was difficult, I began to change my life in small ways. I read scriptures, I covenanted to eat healthy meals, and I promised to sleep for seven to eight hours in each twenty-four-hour period. At first, these few changes were hard to keep. I invited a friend (a spiritual guide) to assist with accountability. I met with her weekly and received support, feedback, and affirmation. I worked with a group twice a week and went out dancing three times a year with them. My church family was essential to my maintenance of sanity. They presented a venue to struggle, vent, and be real in the rawness of grief. Running has given me life and life abundant. It has allowed me to breathe.

God of our every breath,

When it feels like there are not enough hours in a day, give us rest.

When our children keep growing way too fast and time is flying by, help us to cherish each moment.

May we remember that we must also take care of our hearts and minds. Help us to catch our breath and to find rest in you. Fill us with your peace, and may we know that with each breath we take, we breathe in your Spirit.

Dwell in us, Holy Spirit.
Pour into us so that we might be energized and encouraged. Amen.

Rev. Maggie Proshek

Part two

Let's Talk About

Your
Kids

5 Your Child Will Not Be First in Everything, and That is OK

But he said to me, "My grace is sufficient for you, for power is made perfect in weakness." So, I will boast all the more gladly of my weaknesses, so that the power of Christ may dwell in me. Therefore I am content with weaknesses, insults, hardships, persecutions, and calamities for the sake of Christ; for whenever I am weak, then I am strong.

2 Corinthians 12:9-10

Be Present in Their Pain

The joy of sports means that every game is a new and unique opportunity for both fun and learning. Kids feel a lot of energy around games and their outcomes. But that also means losing can be hard. Freezing at a piano recital, getting on the B team, not making the team, third chair in band or orchestra, not making the drill team. Each situation will be challenging. Here is what you need to hear. You will feel the disappointment of your child enormously. You will want to run to the school, coach, or gym and let them know what a mistake they are making. At this moment, you need to pause. Take a deep breath, and take a step back.

Here is what has helped me:

- I have already been in _____ grade. It is now my child's turn.
- I am here to support, not to save or rescue.
- My emotions are not the spotlight. My child's feelings are.
- Reread the section about the 5-5-5 rule.

Not being first is a part of life forever. The job promotions that you don't get, the jobs you don't get, the long-term relationship that ended, these are part of the lessons we learn in growing as a human being. Your child must learn how to deal with disappointment in healthy ways now so that he or she can also do so as an adult.

As a parent, it's never comfortable to see your kids hurting, especially when you can't fix it or them. When your kid is sad or in pain, the best thing you can do is sit with them. Sitting with your kids and letting them process situations can yield some of the most profound lessons in parenting. I am often amazed at the perspective and wisdom my children hold.

I will never forget our younger son's first guitar recital. It was the first time he played a solo in front of a large crowd. He was probably about eleven, and the nerves on this kid were all over the place. His fear made me a nervous wreck. Here is where we must stop trying to control the situation and allow life to happen. I knew that this recital could be a colossal flop. He could get on stage and walk off in tears. He could get on stage and perform just an OK version of the song. He could walk on stage and rock out the place. Each situation can be viewed as a good lesson to be learned. Our role as parents is to give them the space to be nervous, work through it, and come out on the other end.

Prepare now for when they don't make the team, don't get the part in a play, don't get a lead part on the dance team, or go from starter on the team to third string. This pain is real for your child, and it stings just as much for you. It can be surprising how much it hurts to watch your child's disappointment. This will be a time where you cannot just fix it. Do you know what you can do? Sit with them in their disappointment.

Listen to their fears, anger, sadness. Show them how to hold their heads high and congratulate those who got what they were striving for. These moments are golden in their lives, especially for you as parents. You have the honor of being with them, guiding them to move on in a positive way so that one day when they don't get the promotion, make the grade in college, or get the new corner office, they know healthy and appropriate ways to respond.

Moments like the ones listed below for parents can be challenging in the moment but valuable as far as the length and quality of your relationship as parent and child:

- Allowing for the "You're so mean" after a family dispute.
- Driving them to get ice cream after a breakup.
- Validating your child's frustrations during a fight between friends.
- Listening to them playing music to illustrate how they feel.
- Giving them a hug that helps them heal.
- Acknowledging that their silence can be both painful and healing.

There are so many moments like this, which, in the moment, are challenging. During times like these, we as parents wish we could do quick fixes for our kids. But the quick fixes are not helpful. Most of them can be more hurtful in the long run. Sitting with their pain and listening to how they are going to move past it is a gift you can give them that they will never forget, the gift of relationship.

You know as a parent that what is powerful will make them whole. When we fix their problems for them or try to eliminate their pain, we are telling our children they can't handle life themselves. It may feel hard for us to watch, but our kids are resilient. They can do hard things.

Effort vs. Reward

Our kids can do hard things. They can. I struggled in school as a child, especially when it came to things I had to spell or memorize. My mom worked with me, my teachers worked with me, I got tested, got tutors, and then I realized that I should never enter the spelling bee. I studied and studied for a spelling test, vocab test, and test where you had to memorize things, and still I struggled. I worked hard to get good or at least acceptable grades. Let's look at effort vs. reward when it comes to grades. Then we can place this model into other life situations. But there are times where you, as the parent, also need to connect with the teacher.

If your child is struggling in a class and you see the effort behind his or her work, you have several questions to ask yourself:

1) Is your child paying attention in class?
2) How is the teacher teaching (maybe the teaching style is not your kids' number-one learning style)?
3) Is your child doing homework or practicing the skills necessary to succeed?
4) Is your child communicating with the teacher?
5) Is your child going to tutoring?
6) Have you communicated with the teacher?

I need to say here that starting in middle school, I believe the first forms of communication need to be initiated by the student. It is a great life skill for them to find ways to be their own advocate. But there are times where you, as the parent, also need to connect with the teacher.

If you or your student can answer yes to many of the questions above, and the grade is still not what you expect, this is when I lean heavily on the value of effort vs. reward. If you are working hard for a B or C, then I would take that B or C and recognize the industry behind it. If you are not working toward an acceptable grade, then consequences may be necessary.

Here is where parenting is yet again a balancing game of looking at your child and the situation, and then determining if it is your place to help and encourage or allow for consequences. This effort vs. reward balance will be different for each child you have and will probably change as they get older. We all know that just when we start to get our parenting thing down to a great routine, things change, and we have to pivot.

Is it OK to Quit?

Is it OK to quit a team? By definition, a team is a group in which your effort matters. Your input affects others. For example, if you are a member of a band and you don't practice, the whole band will be affected. That said, all newly acquired skills may seem horrible at first. We have lived through two middle school band instruments, guitar, moving from coach pitch to kid pitch in baseball, middle school football, and high school geometry. Any new skill takes a lot of work. This means it's easy to stop. Our rule was that if you committed to a team, you had to commit for the season or the school year and put forth the effort. Then you could see how it felt in the end. And yet, there are always exceptions to rules. If the coach and your kid have a personality conflict, is it better to work through it? Or is it better to end it? If music isn't your kid's thing and it's putting extraordinary strain and stress on him or her, is it OK to quit? These are questions you must ask yourself in your own family. Each family has a different rhythm and a different scale for when it's OK to stop doing something.

I will say teaching our kids to work hard toward something is not as easy as it sounds. So is it OK to quit a team sometimes? Sometimes yes, sometimes no. Do you need to stick it out and be a team player? Sometimes yes, sometimes no. I interviewed one of our boy's coaches, and he has a great perspective about what success looks like in sports. It's not always winning the game, being on the first team, or being a starting player. It's the person who is a great teammate. It's learning the skills of endurance. It's encouraging others. It's putting others before yourself. It's helping your teammate up when they're down. Learning to work within a team is a valuable lesson.

The bottom line of this chapter is that you know your kid's best effort. You know when they need to be pushed and encouraged, and you know when enough is enough. Be honest with yourself and your child, and you will move forward with the best plan for your family.

Parenting Perspective: Rev. Dr. Terry Parsons
Parent, Pastor, Counselor

Do you remember the bumper sticker on the cars of proud parents that read, "My child is an honor student at XYZ School"? At that time, our daughter was an honor student, and our son with ADHD and dyslexia was not. Then, I was delighted to later see a bumper sticker that read, "I am glad that my child is passing at XYZ School." It made me smile.

A woman I see in therapy is an executive with a

major corporation and has two children, a twelve-year-old son and an eight-year-old daughter. The family went to an Air B&B during a school break. The house was filled with the owner's children's first-place trophies, and the children's rooms were plastered with posters: "Only Winners in This Family," "I Am Number One," "Tops in My Class," and "1600 SAT." My client asked, "Are we not pushing our children enough?"

Can you imagine the pressure these children felt? There is nothing wrong with wanting the best for your children, but to place such ultimate expectations on a child can potentially create a plethora of problems.

As a psychology professional, parent, and now grandparent, I share with you in the joys and challenges of being a parent. Each child is a unique and changing kaleidoscope of multiple traits and characteristics. Each child is multifaceted and can change dramatically in an ever-morphing developmental process. What an adventure for both child and parent!

I am using the term *adventure* rather than *journey,* because one of my former students made a distinction that stayed with me. He said, "I think of a journey as having a destination in mind. An adventure means you do not necessarily know where you are going. That means there are some knowns and a lot of unknowns that make the process more interesting, exciting, sometimes scary, and a continuous learning experience." As you can attest, parenting is indeed an adventure, because each child is different.

Some children are self-motivated and other children need a nudge, more structure, or extra help. Some children are naturally gifted in one or several areas while other children struggle to keep up or even to just make it. You can see the variety in your own personal experience, in your family of origin, and in your present family.

What did your parents or growing-up environment expect of you? Were you always first? How did you deal with not always being first? What did you learn about yourself and how you coped? How does your child deal with not being first? These experiences can be helpful topics for discussion.

It is important to read the literature, listen to podcasts, and learn from the "experts" about being a good parent. But it is vital to be a student of your unique child. You observe, listen to, note responses and interests, see the personality traits and emotional reactions, check social qualities and learning styles, and keep current with the various developmental processes of this amazing gift to your life. Being a parent is quite a learning experience. I believe we usually learn by trial and error rather than wins and losses.

Some parents only recognize winning and high levels of achievement and scoff at "participation trophies." Other parents go overboard in rewarding every little deed or assignment.

Loving, accepting, and valuing your child in ways that foster a sense of security and well-being help the child to know that life is not just performance-based. This helps the child not to carry the anxious and insecure feeling of "I'm not good enough if I am not the best."

Teach and encourage your child that the qualities of putting forth effort, trying your best, and figuring things out are rewarding in and of themselves. Help your child learn the values of faith, the courage to try new things, respect, kindness, compassion, how to overcome challenges and disappointments, perseverance, wonder and curiosity, healthy relationships and good people skills, and to develop their own unique interests and meaningful accomplishments. These are some of the most important qualities to develop and celebrate.

It is a mathematical fact that in any group of two or more, there will only be one number one. Strive for number one if that is important, but the odds are much greater that this will not be the case. So, enjoy the qualities and not just the numbers.

A common coaching or parenting principle says, "Success is not about wins and losses. It is about helping these young people become their best selves on and off the field."

A self-described "Type A personality and always compete to win" dad shared with me a personal story about going on a camping and fishing trip with his seven-year-old son. He said, "These other dads and sons were just pulling in the fish. I was getting really upset because neither of us had caught one fish. I did not want my son to feel like we were losers. Finally, each of us caught one fish. I apologized to my son, but he said that he had a great time and that he really enjoyed our time of being together. I learned an important parenting lesson."

Knowing that your child will not be first at everything is crucial for healthy parenting. This is a vital life lesson for your child to learn to cope, enjoy, and navigate in the world.

Dear God,

Sometimes I feel sad when I don't win. I don't like when I lose, but it's OK if I do because no matter if I lose or win, I can still have a good day. It's OK that I lose because I am still part of a team, and we did our best. Amen.

Spencer and Collin Jewell (9 and 6 years old)

Parent Prayer

God,

Please help me support my children when they don't succeed. It is hard in the moment to see them fail, but I know that growth can happen from those moments of disappointment. Give me the strength to let them make mistakes, and the courage to not sweep in to solve their problems. Make them perfect in their weakness and gracious in their wins. Amen.

Erin Jewell

6   Your Kids Need Room to Grow

For even when we were with you, we gave you this command: Anyone unwilling to work should not eat. For we hear that some of you are living in idleness, mere busybodies, not doing any work. Now such persons we command and exhort in the Lord Jesus Christ to do their work quietly and to earn their own living.

2 Thessalonians 3:10-12

Tying Shoes and Other Life Skills

In preparation for this section, I did an internet search for kids' shoes. In my search, I discovered that approximately 80 percent of kids' shoes did not have laces. They had Velcro, stretchy openings, or fake laces, but kids' shoes with laces were hard to find. I was a first- and second-grade teacher for several years before the shoe companies started with the no-laces trend. The most popular kid in first grade was the one who could zip a zipper and tie shoes! These life skills could get you far in a first-grade classroom. But the gift of tying a shoe and zipping a zipper meant that parents had to build in twenty to thirty minutes of prep time before they had to leave the house so that their kids could dress themselves. Learning how to tie a shoe is frustrating. It takes time and some patience, but when you have that skill, it is yours forever. It does not go away.

Parents of toddlers or even children under six years old know that YOU can dress your kid in about two to three minutes. THEY can dress themselves in twenty to thirty minutes. Those twenty to thirty minutes can feel like a lifetime of awfulness; but honestly, when they are so proud that they pulled their pants up or put their socks on, it is worth it! When my kids were young, I would bring them into my bedroom or bathroom, put their clothing on the floor, and then I would finish my hair and makeup so that we were getting ready together. In the twenty minutes it took me to get dressed, brush my teeth, fix my hair, and put on some makeup, they got on one sock and half a T-shirt, but at least we were getting somewhere.

Learning skills that will help your kids in life is essential. It is not easy, but it is important. As parents, you need to keep your eye on today. But the greater perspective of our job is to let them learn to live. I always say that I am raising good roommates and partners. I want my children to know how to live and work with others, how to order a pizza and give a good tip. I want them to love God and their neighbors. If I can do that, and only that, I will know they can see the world through others' eyes, have perspective, have empathy, and just be good people. Learning life skills can all start with learning how to tie a shoe. Remember to take your time and go slow.

Learning a new skill is not easy. The skills we want to learn, we first see done by experts. We would never want to play the piano if we saw a child learning the first scales. No, we look to a master who can play unique pieces that give us chills. But, to get to the place to play unique pieces, we must first learn the scales. When it comes to learning to tie a shoe, it can feel like everyone in the world knows how to do this "simple" skill, but the child is learning how to accomplish it for the very first time.

Learning to tie a shoe is hard. It is frustrating, but man, when you get it, when it clicks, that is joy and pride! And that skill is just one of a thousand life skills that your child will need to have so that one day he or she will be able to live a productive and positive life without you.

Below is a list of some of the skills your kids will need to master during their various phases of growth. All the skills below fall into the categories of communication, critical thinking, self-control, and resilience. These are the skills that we want to build in our children. We foster them by teaching them little things along the way that grow into more important things. Someday, they will turn into full-grown adults who can pay bills, make appointments, get jobs, and have fulfilling relationships with others.

Early Childhood

Taking plates to the sink

Putting toys in baskets

Putting clothes in hampers

Dressing (with some assistance)

Mastering zippers, ties, and buttons

Younger Elementary

Picking out clothes for the week

Knowing essential phone numbers and addresses

Helping with packing lunches

Brushing teeth and hair

Vacuuming

Dusting

Helping with cooking (mixing, measuring, and pouring)

Setting and cleaning the table

Ordering a meal at a restaurant (maybe with some help)

Upper Elementary

Packing lunches

Doing laundry

Doing household chores

Making simple meals

Ordering a meal

Making a schedule or plan for the week (school, events, and chores)

Middle School

Staying at home alone

Going into a store to purchase items (making lists, making change)

Creating tasks and completing them by a due date

Ironing clothing

Putting air in tires

High School

Developing job interview skills

Keeping a calendar updated

Pumping gas

Knowing how to tip

Getting a job

Creating a budget

This is not a complete list, but it gives you an idea of the bigger picture and of how perspective can change, depending upon the age and characteristics of your kids. You don't need your toddler out pumping gas for you. In fact, that would be inappropriate. But your toddler can buckle his or her seatbelt, carry a backpack, and say hello to others. These small skills build upon one another to build confidence, critical thinking, and relationship skills, and these skills help your child to grow into a confident and self-reliant adult.

Encourage Freedom, Develop Responsibility

The balance between freedom and responsibility is a hard one to find. This is the type of thing where the finish line is always moving. We want to have children who grow into self-sufficient adults. This book is helping you gain perspective. If you look at the infant child in your arms and fast forward to them driving a car and getting an apartment, it can freeze you in your tracks. This is a parenting piece that is better when you have the long-term goal in mind yet take this one moment at a time.

The definition of freedom with children is very different depending on family systems, social norms, and your own comfort as a parent. So, you need to find in your own house what your limits and expectations are. You must start allowing some freedoms for your child so that they can develop responsibility. I believe that developing responsibility can and should start young.

For younger children you can communicate and model responsibility. Our children are learning from us in how we act and respond in our own lives. As you are going about your day with your younger children begin giving them some choices. As you are giving choices, as the adult, make sure they are all things that fit into your expectations. For example, you can ask your child if they would like an apple or some pretzels for a snack, what music they want to dance to, what shirt they want to wear that day, what book they want to read before bed. This allows them to think and choose (responsibility) and move forward. Let your children help you accomplish things around the house, such as cooking, picking up, and so on. This will take some more time in the beginning, yet when they become teenagers and they are able to help you fully clean your house, mow the lawn, and cook dinner you will be grateful and proud.

As they get older you can help communicate how different

choices can create different outcomes. You made the choice today to rush through homework, which resulted in mistakes. Now we need to do it again. It is also vital to point out positive choices and reinforce these behaviors. This will encourage the positive behaviors to continue. As children get older, some of the shift of responsibility is playing outside alone, walking home from school, gaining access to technology, and so on. Again, each next step is going to differ by community and your own house expectations. As I have pointed out it is important to manage expectations of responsibility. When you start asking your child to put their own laundry away, it will not be as organized as when you did it, but it will be done.

In our house we did not pay our children for doing house responsibilities. This was an expectation for each person living in the house to take care of it. You do you, but make sure the responsibility being completed is not done solely for a reward. It is completed because that is what is necessary and right.

I joke that my goal is to have children who one day will make a good roommate/spouse. They need to be able to communicate with others, pick up after themselves, do a load of laundry, problem solve, and pivot.

Offer Options, Not Solutions

As you are developing responsibility in your children, it is natural to tell them how to do it. We are really fixers by nature. We see a problem or a struggle and we want to be able to help fix it in the most effective way possible. When parenting, if we don't allow for struggle and problem solving, we are not helping our children, just our own schedule. The other piece of this is that if we offer different options for our children, they still get to find the best way to solve something.

Problem-solving is something that we use every day of our lives. Developing this skill can be painful for parents and children but well worth the time. Can you imagine doing your life today without having made mistakes, making decisions, learning to pivot and move to a new solution?

When children are struggling with something they will typically want to seek a quick solution. If we are honest, we as adults also seek a quick solution to problems. Yet, as parents we do best for our children when we offer them different options, paths to move forward. I like to say, would you like to hear about how other people might deal with this?

Here is the thing: some days you just tell them what to do and move on. But, most days you take the time to offer ways to help so that they are the ones who can take the time and problem-solve, to be the heroes of their situations. When we give the right way and do all the thinking, we become the heroes. Parenting our children is all about them, and some about us. I have often told my kids, "I have already completed third grade. It is your turn."

This is also about how to react to a situation. Our children have choices to respond with grace, kindness, and an open perspective *or* to respond with frustration and anger. As children develop social and cognitive minds, they are also developing their relationship with Christ. This profound connection can also help guide and encourage our children to make good choices, to lean into the faith that we have given them and begin to make it their own. This is also done by offering options, telling stories of our faith, learning how people for over two thousand years have had to grow and learn, and how we are given that opportunity in a social and spiritual way.

Like I said before and will continue to say again, we are

here to advocate and help our children grow. This is done best, at any age, by offering options and allowing them to figure out the problem. They can do this, and so can you.

Parenting Perspective: Dr. Brad Schwall
Parent, Counselor

What is our purpose as parents? Our goal is to equip and nurture our children so that they may be caring, loving, and resilient adults. Ultimately, they will live on their own. We are guiding, teaching, and redirecting their lives in order that someday they will develop a sense of self and independence. Throughout parenting, we must make decisions about when to step in and when to step back. When our children are young, we prevent problems. We cover electrical outlets. We create a safe environment for babies beginning to crawl. As our children get older, we facilitate playdates at which we still provide supervision to ensure a safe and pleasant time. When our children reach the school years. We have less and less control over their behavior.

The teenage years present new challenges as more freedom is given even before all executive functioning skills have fully developed. Our teens are driving. Yet their prefrontal cortex is not fully developed. Our children are bound to make mistakes. We are presented with the dilemma of how to respond when our children get into predicaments, have to face natural consequences, and back themselves into a corner. Challenges that we don't know how to respond to as parents include when our kids get cut from the team, try to deal with relational conflict, or simply forget their homework at home. When our child faces either consequences or disappointments, we must remember our purpose as parents. Our goal is to encourage the development of discernment, self-awareness, and responsibility in decision-making. We must first stop, listen to our child, and then assess the situation and its ramifications. Let your child describe the problem. Reflect feelings your child may be having. Help your child identify the problem and his or her role in that problem. Validate rational disappointment about unmet expectations. Decide who owns the problem. Is the situation a result of poor choices? Is your child facing disappointment over a circumstance out of her or his control? We have a continuum of possible responses. Direct input may be needed. Our input may model appropriate responses. We may need to listen and facilitate our child's problem-solving. This helps our child develop his or her own solutions and responses. How do we know when to become directly involved? Is the situation detrimental to your child's well-being? Or is the situation conducive to your child speaking up for himself or herself? Is your child facing a natural consequence that may become a lesson?

When we rescue our children, we are undermining their ability to self-direct as well as their confidence in being able to problem-solve and advocate for themselves, to respond responsibly. Coming up with a solution ourselves or immediately intervening implies that our child cannot do it for himself or herself. This establishes a pattern of enabling. In life, we learn that there are consequences for actions. Life is never without disappointments or setbacks. We learn how to grieve, be resilient, and have hope. When we face disappointment, we must be in tune with our feelings and accept what we cannot change. Facing disappointment happens throughout life. We learn how to look for the positive and grow through those setbacks. Intervening to remove a disappointment in our child's life inhibits the opportunity for them to learn these skills. It is difficult to see our children hurting. We want the best for them. The best may not be an immediate and short-term relief, but it is this continued growth through challenges and disappointments that will prepare our children for a life of choices, changes, and challenges.

Gracious and glorious God,

*I don't know how you do it. I don't get how you can be love
because it seems too risky.*

*There are days I am afraid to love with my whole heart
for fear of it breaking. I don't know if I can face that kind of pain.
So, I protect my heart from the potential of grief.
And then I feel guilty about putting up walls.*

*But you know how costly love is. And even when I am behind walls
of fear and doubt, you love me.*

*Help me find strength in the love you always show us—
"We love because God first loved us."
All the love I have comes from you.*

*Help me to extend the same love I give to others to myself.
Love will hurt sometimes, but your love remains steadfast.
Empower me to hold on to your love. Because you show us
how to love first, in you I have the capacity to love more
than I give myself credit for. Amen.*

Rev. Jennifer Chickering

7

Your Kids' Mistakes Do Not Define Who They Are

Don't worry about anything; instead, pray about everything. Tell God what you need, and thank him for all he has done. Then you will experience God's peace, which exceeds anything we can understand. His peace will guard your hearts and minds as you live in Christ Jesus.

Philippians 4:6-7 NLT

Little Mistakes Can Help Eliminate Big Mistakes

The best way to let your kids fail is with a net. I don't think we can hear this often enough as parents. Letting them fall (read: fail) when they know they have the safety net of your care, compassion, and love is so important. The trick is not to rescue them but to support them. Here is a simple example that happened in our house. As our children gained the responsibility for smartphones, they also had to live into the rules and expectations of being online and using social media. We gave a smartphone to one of our boys at the Christmas of his fifth-grade year. (Let me pause the story by saying that there are many different opinions and approaches to technology and children. I am not saying this is the only way. I am saying this is what we did). OK, so kiddo got a phone in December of his fifth grade year. We laid out our technology rules as follows:

- You cannot have your phone in your room at night.
- You must charge your phone on the family charging station.
- Parents will know all the passwords for all your technology

and apps.

- We will look at and monitor all communications.
- You cannot follow anyone whom we have not invited into our home. (Exceptions can be made with parent approval.)

These guidelines defined the basic rules of phone use in our house. We started small, and our son got on one social media platform. We allowed him to follow a show that he liked. A few weeks later, we noticed that he had followed all of the fan pages about that show, some of them OK, some of them not OK. This was a fantastic opportunity to allow a little mistake to be a big lesson. The lessons learned were these: You have choices in life, and choices have repercussions, sometimes good, sometimes bad. In this situation, we all learned together and moved on. The use of social media can have real consequences, big ones. Learning lessons from simple mistakes can help limit the possibility of much more significant mistakes—and the consequences that follow.

The mistake he made was not following the rules and guidelines that we set as a family to use social media. The repercussions on our son's life for this mistake were almost zero. I will say at the time when consequences were handed out, it felt huge. I don't remember exactly what the result was, but I assume, no phone and no social media for a time.

That said, things that feel big at the time can feel small in the future. Anytime that you have disappointment in your life, it can feel monumental.

A mistake, by definition, means that you're mistaken, and nobody likes to be incorrect. But guess what? We are all wrong at some time or another. We all make mistakes. My mom likes to say that it is our humanity showing through. I had a friend in my office this past week who noticed that I had misspelled

January and February on my wall calendars. I have two degrees, and I still can't seem to spell correctly. I hate it. It embarrasses me so very much. Yet, I should have known that I have spelling issues and used one of the three smart devices in my office to check it. But, no. I just threw some letters on the wall and acted like I did not care. This is partly because we were still in the middle of a pandemic, and very few people were in my office. Yet at that moment, when she told me that my words were misspelled, I felt shame. She did not make me feel guilt, but it came. I felt my cheeks get red. I made some joke about being dyslexic, and then I changed them as fast as I could! This is a silly example of a mistake that is no big deal, yet at that moment, it felt like a big deal.

The point that I'm hoping to make is that no matter how big or how small a mistake is, it can feel big. It can feel overwhelming. It can feel like you can't get past it. But you can. And your kid can. So, at that moment, in the middle of the mistake, the disappointment, the fear, the shame, stop, take a breath, and recognize that you are strong enough to move past this and to move through this. Some mistakes are significant. Some mistakes can get us expelled from school, get us thrown in jail, or make us lose the trust of some loved ones. There are many consequences to mistakes. But you get to choose how you're going to respond to the mistake. Can we own up again, accept it and apologize for it, and move on and better ourselves from it? Are you going to make it a life lesson so that the next time you choose to do XYZ, stop and remember the pain that it caused before? You can do this as an adult, and you can help your child do this too. Addressing little mistakes can prevent big mistakes and help our children understand that mistakes are not who we are; they are just how we acted in that moment. They do not need to define us.

Recognize the mistake but love the child. This is something that is not always easy. Most mistakes that are made today by our children are in the public spectrum. Even if it was private initially, soon the stories, pictures, and videos are all over different social media platforms. This gives your child the ability to relive this mistake again and again. So, turn off the phone and take time together. Now, we all realize that turning off the phone will not turn off social media. But these little times where we understand that we can turn it off to help gain perspective is real. When we make children turn off the phone or ground them from technology, they stop it, but it is not their choice. But asking them if they want to step away from it for a while is different. They can spend this time thinking about how they can deal with the different social media outlets that are in their lives. I am not an expert with technology and kids, but I do know that giving them skills to learn how to cope with the phone will serve you all well. This is something that is constantly changing. Technology is far from stagnant, it is more like a high-speed train that you are riding on. So, name the mistake, look your child in the eye, and remind your child that your love for him or her is more significant than any mistake. Loving your child through a mistake does not mean that there are no consequences. It shows them that they are loved fully. I have an expression that I use with my family, "I love you every moment of every day, and I like you most of them."

When the Principal Calls

Listen. Learn. Advocate when necessary. That is a motto I try to follow.

In one of the first nine weeks of high school, we got a phone call that our son was being sent to in-school suspension (ISS). The reason why boiled down to some miscommunication and misunderstanding. But it was what it was. This was a kid who had never been to the principal's office before, and here he was in ISS for three days. Of course, I was out of town. I got the call from my husband letting me know the details. As a mom at that moment, I wanted to protect my child, from making it better to fixing all the things and fixing them quickly. Instead, I listened to the story from my husband. I then heard the story from my son. My husband and I talked it over and set up a meeting with the principal to clear up a few things. We decided to advocate for our son. We told our side, our opinions, and listened to the administration's side and views. In the end, we had to agree to disagree. We could have taken this to the school board and fought the decision.

I am not sure what the outcome would have been, but we decided to move on. My son is functioning fine today. He served his three days in ISS. There were no blinking lights that followed him wherever he went letting people know that he was suspended from school. He liked the quiet working environment. He got some rest, and he got to catch up on schoolwork. It wasn't entirely a bad thing. Yet at the moment when we got the phone call from the school, it felt huge. The week following, it felt huge. But living out the consequence didn't break him. Today as I'm writing about it, I get a little smile on my face when I think back to all the drama that ensued after that phone call, all the tears (from me, not my child), and all the anger and stress. The situation turned into a life lesson for all of us.

It is OK to be upset when mistakes happen. You can feel all the feelings. You can be disappointed in your kids or in your kids' friends. You need to remember that you did not make a mistake. For each life stage your child is in, there can be different responses, but for all of them, remember this is not about you. This is a choice your child made. For each stage, you ask the question, "Can I help you with this?" Or "What do you think you should do next?" This allows your child to accept responsibility, make amends, and move on with a life lesson intact.

Here are some other examples of similar life lessons where you as a parent can help your child learn how to be an advocate for themselves. They can learn how to stop and say sorry. This is also an opportunity for you to listen, learn, and advocate when necessary, allowing your children to take the lead. When we allow natural consequences to play out, learning happens and our children gain confidence, empathy, and trust in themselves. This is a life still worth taking time to develop.

Early Childhood
Mistake: Hitting a sibling
Response: How can we use words when we are angry? Give your child an appropriate time out and then work toward an apology to said sibling. Then when time out is done, move on, give hugs and love.

Elementary
Mistake: Got into trouble at school for talking when asked to stop. (There are so many options here.)
Response: Listen to your child about what happened. Ask if there could have been a better response. Develop a consequence for home. Show love. Move on.

Middle School
Mistake: Did not turn in a major assignment and is now failing

the class.

Response: Talk about the importance of setting schedules and calendars. Listen. Ask if your child needs help in the class, or was it a mistake. Are they overwhelmed with the assignment or did they just not complete it. Develop a consequence for home. Show love. Move on.

High School

Mistake: Your child got a ticket for driving too fast.

Response: Listen to the situation. Talk about the importance of driving safely. Develop a consequence for home. Show love. Move on.

College

Mistake: Did not pay rent on time, now has a late fee, and now their bank account is at $0.00.

Response: Listen to the situation. Ask if you can give some advice or if they want to vent. Life has already given the consequence. Show love. Move on.

Each situation above has been simplified. The emotions have been taken out. The disappointment, the fear, all the things that can happen when people feel worried and stressed. What I want you to understand is that no matter what stage your child is in, they will make mistakes. You need to listen, address the mistake and how to fix it, show love, and move on. Parents need to advocate only when necessary, or sometimes ask the right questions, but as much as possible, allow natural consequences to play out, and allow children to figure things out for themselves. Talking things through is a good way to help your child process. This allows you to be there for them but not to solve the problem for them.

Sex, Drugs, and Rock and Roll

Each life stage has challenges, and middle school and high school (yes, middle school) can be filled with temptations of nicotine, drugs, and sex. If you think back to your high school days, you either experimented yourself or knew people who did. Or maybe you did not. But today, most middle school and high school students are faced with these temptations.

Please talk to your children about nicotine, drugs, and sex before you need to. I am a firm believer that knowledge is real power, and if you can give your children knowledge for each topic that does not come from peers or social media platforms, you will provide your children power. Have honest and open conversations about the temptations and consequences before they happen and develop trust in your family for when hard questions might need to be asked.

This is not easy. Looking at your sweet young child and letting them into some dark sides of the world seems a little counterintuitive. But the alternative is allowing strangers and peers to do the education for you. That can be downright scary.

In our family, we have a family code word that our kids can say or text, and that means that we will call and say they need to come home. My boys have used it at times. Most of the time, it was not to get out of a horrible situation. They just did not want to spend the night and did not want to hurt a friend's feelings. My husband and I never cared about being the bad guy to our kids' friends. Each time our kids have used our code word, the first two seconds after I read it, my heart rate went up, and I have had horrible images of what type of situation they were needing to get out of. Again, most of the time, it was that they wanted to come home. The time may come, though, when they don't want to be at a party where everyone is taking shots or doing drugs, and all they need to do is text our code word, and they get to come home.

I urge you to educate yourself about this teenage phase of parenting and your child about their possible temptations. When our boys were in middle school, the fad was vaping. Everyone was vaping. Guess what I did? I went to our local vape store and asked the person to show and tell me everything about vaping. I learned what different vapes looked like, smelled like, and how kids concealed them. When I went to this store, I had zero worries that my kids were vaping, but I also knew that about 60 percent of teenagers were, which meant a high probability that our kids would encounter it. So, I educated myself and then was able to educate my kids. I took power away from something that I knew little about through my own education.

I am not an addiction expert or counselor. If you suspect that your child may be dealing with a serious issue, please get the advice of an expert who knows the difference between experimentation and addiction, and get your child and your family the proper help for your situation. But I do know that even "good" kids will sometimes do "bad" things. This might be staying out past curfew, smoking a joint with a friend, or getting drunk one night. It happens. This is when you as a parent need to pay attention, set healthy boundaries and expectations, provide space to your kids, and pay more attention. As a parent, we always want to think the best of our kids, and in that same vein, our kids don't want us to know when they mess up. So, what can happen? When kids make a mistake with drugs or alcohol, parents tend to choose one of two paths: overreact or underreact. We don't want to see that our kid is doing drugs, so we look the other way. Or we find out that our child smoked weed, and we become Fort Knox. Life is always a balance. You will need to find yours.

At the start of this chapter, we read Philippians 4:6-7: "Don't worry about anything; instead, pray about everything. Tell God what you need, and thank him for all he has done. Then you will experience God's peace, which exceeds anything we can understand. His peace will guard your hearts and minds as you live in Christ Jesus." This Bible verse has been one that I often say in my parenting journey. The first sentence gives me an option: I can worry, or I can pray. I choose to pray. I can be angry, or I can recognize the goodness in my life. I chose goodness. I can be afraid or lean into the peace from God. I choose peace.

Parenting Perspective: Rev. Dr. Pam White
Parent, Pastor, Counselor

Our identity is important. I use the word identity to refer to who we are at our core. Although it sometimes takes us a while to discern who we understand ourselves to be, and to connect with this deeper reality, our identity is relatively unchanging. Our behavior, on the other hand, is a partial expression of who we are at any given moment. In various roles through the years, I have been reminded that these are often two very different things.

In my first career, I was a licensed professional counselor who worked in the area of psychophysiology, looking at the mind/body connection. In this role as a therapist, I often taught about the difference between congruent and incongruent behavior. Something is

---

congruent when it is in agreement or in harmony. Abraham Maslow and other humanistic therapists theorized that the ultimate goal in life is to become self-actualized, which involves becoming our true self. In my practice, I saw that a foundational journey throughout life was the challenge of getting rid of unhealthy, incongruent behavior and moving toward behavior that was more congruent with a person's core identity. My role in this process was to help to modify a client's behavior so that it more fully expressed who they were. Through behavioral modification we worked to eliminate unhealthy behavior patterns. A big part of my practice involved working to reduce stress and anxiety. These unhealthy responses resulted in behaviors that began to mask a person's core identity, and the individual began to identify with the unhealthy behavior. Through therapy, we would go through the critical process of identifying incongruent behavior and putting a plan in place to use behavioral modification to shift toward a more congruent way of living.

After many years in the counseling field, I attended seminary and became an ordained elder in the United Methodist Church. As a pastor, I began to address this same problem through a different lens. I believe that we all are created in God's image but that so much of our behavior is incongruent with this truth. As Christians we seek to more faithfully follow Christ, which means constantly recognizing behavior that gets in the way. Whereas my main goal in therapy was to empower an individual to make this change, as a pastor

I now recognize that this is only part of the equation. We do have to take an active role in eliminating incongruent behavior, but we do not do this alone. The other side of the coin is the belief that God is ever-present in our lives, constantly transforming us so that we can more fully express that core identity. This identity is grounded in the love of Christ, a love that works within us and a love that constantly calls us outside of ourselves to share this love with others. It should be a guiding force for all of our behavior. In theological talk, we refer to behavior that is incongruent with this truth as being sinful. This behavior pulls us off of the path of growing to become more Christlike, and it can create blind spots that keep us from recognizing our core identity. In my ministry I seek to share the love of Christ and help others recognize this light that is within them as I encourage them to grow in their ability to also share this light with others.

I have another role in life, one that is significantly more important than that of therapist or pastor. I am mother to my two daughters. Throughout the years I have done my best to help them learn this lesson. They are young adults now and are learning to spread their wings in the world as they forge their own paths. The most critical task in this stage of life has two elements to it. First, young adults will begin to solidify a sense of identity, and then they make decisions about the expression of this identity through the many choices that they face. This includes big decisions, like those relating to one's vocation and relationships, and smaller decisions, like how to budget and spend money and where to devote time and energy. These are not easy choices to make, and they are rarely made without second-guessing oneself. As a mom, I hope to remind my girls over and over that their stumbles and mistakes do not define who they are. I hope to be a touchstone that regularly points them back to the truth of who they are at their core. They are filled with love and compassion and a desire to make a difference in this world. Whether they perceive that they fail or succeed on any given day, this doesn't change the truth of who they are. They are created and sustained in God's love, and this reality is not altered by a wrong decision or a series of steps on the wrong path. They are more than their behavior, and this means that their mistakes do not define who they are. This is something we all need to be reminded of, over and over.

God,

is my child's worst day connected to lack of faith?
God, help me believe what you believe about my child.
Their worst day does not define who they are.
My child is defined by love that endures, forgives, loves at all times,
and does not keep a record of wrongs (1 Corinthians 13:4-7).
I know that that is how you love me.

My gift to my child in the worst of times
is to intentionally pass God's love through me to him.
In Jesus' name.

Rev. Dr. Lael Melville

PARt three

Let's Talk About

HOW TO WORK TOGETHER

8 You Will Have Dreams for Your Children That They Do Not Share

After looking at the way things are on this earth, here's what I've decided is the best way to live: Take care of yourself, have a good time, and make the most of whatever job you have for as long as God gives you life. And that's about it. That's the human lot. Yes, we should make the most of what God gives, both the bounty and the capacity to enjoy it, accepting what's given and delighting in the work. It's God's gift! God deals out joy in the present, the now. It's useless to brood over how long we might live.

Ecclesiastes 5:18-20 MSG

We All Want a Healthy Baby

The reality of parenting can be very hard. I will never forget one night with one of our children when we were up all hours of the night doing breathing treatments. The kid was crying. I was crying. At that moment, I remember thinking, "This is what I have been dreaming and praying for? This is pretty horrible." Then I felt guilt. Then I probably fell asleep.

Parenting is a skill. It takes time to learn and develop. Here is the trickiest thing about parenting. Once you feel like you have mastered a skill, you will need to learn a new one. I know some people who have a hobby habit. They would try tennis, basketball, piano, flute, whatever they could find. Until something fit. The reality of new skills is that it takes time and effort to make it look easy.

When choosing a new hobby, it is typically because we have seen an expert at a game or in a concert. But the result we are looking at came from many years of hard work.

The reality of being a parent comes fast. You have nine months to prepare. You can read books, set up the perfect nursery, get all the baby things you can find, but your baby will still cry, and you won't know how to comfort him or her. You will feed him, burp him, change him, rock her, drive her, walk her, sway her, but he or she might still be crying at the end of all of it. If you are dealing with this stage now, you are not alone. I genuinely believe that this is why babies are so cute. The next day, they will half-smile at you, and it all feels worth it.

So, what do you do when it is hard? You take some time to gain some perspective. You take a deep breath. I am a very firm believer that perspective and parenting must go hand in hand. So, let's look at a few examples:

- Your baby is crying. The baby is alive. If the baby is crying, that is good. He or she is developing healthy lungs and could be an Olympic swimmer one day. The baby will not cry forever.
- Your toddler learns the word *no* and uses it all the time. Your toddler has the cognitive ability to use language. He or she will soon learn other words too.
- Your elementary age child is struggling in school, and each night, the homework hour turns into a battle of wills. Your child is learning to do hard things. He is also learning that you will sit with him in the hard times.
- Your middle school child is listening to your peers and ignoring all the things that come out of your mouth. This is a natural progression. Your child must learn to connect with other adults outside of the house.
- Your high school child experiences a heartbreak and seems broken and fragile. She is still under your roof. You

can model and love her through it so that she will be stronger on the other side.

I know these are simple examples of hard times, but what I want you to see in it is that in the brokenness, in the hard times, there can be another story when you get to the end. I am not here to tell you that it is all going to work out with a perfect bow in the future. It will not. Parenting is a skill in which you learn as you go with live subject matter.

I find it helpful to surround myself with people in different parenting stages to give me the best support system. When I talk to grandparents, it is great to see the perspective of joy that grandkids have in their lives. The empty-nester family who is learning to create a new rhythm with adult children, the parent of teens who, at this time, are my people, remind me that we can do hard things. The parents of elementary children who are starting to see their child's personalities blossom. The parents of young children who sing the silly songs and do the silly dances also need to be assured that their children will feed and bathe themselves one day.

Your Expectations Will Be Challenged

As parents of young children, we engaged in several different sports teams with our children. We have boys who have an above average body build, and they are typically very coachable. This can be a great asset to a team. This is what I am learning as I live into my uncharted role as a mom of athletes. I grew up in a family with a sister, and we were in band and theater, church choir, and played some soccer as kids, but sports were never a rhythm in our household. My husband grew up in a family with all boys. They played sports and watched sports. Now we have kids with their own expectations and experiences they'd like to try. Which do we do?

I have found that when it comes to our kids' activities, it's not so much about which ones they choose but about how many they choose. While they need to have the freedom to pursue their desired activities, we also as a family need to decide on how much we can comfortably fit into our schedule and calendar. If there is any advice I wished I had listened to as a young mom, it was this: you don't have to engage your children in every possible activity in order for them to grow and experience life. Let them find one thing at a time, and give it a chance. I see so many young families driving to soccer, piano, karate, and voice lessons, all in the course of a week. But when you take on this kind of schedule, there is no time to truly enjoy that activity, whatever it may be.

In our lives, we did one outside thing per season or semester. This rule came out of doing too much at the start. We did not plan to overschedule our children. It just happened. We joined Cub Scouts with some friends. We put one kid on a soccer team and the other on another soccer team. We were in the church choir, did piano lessons, and volunteered. Let's look at what happened to our family calendar.

Monday: soccer practice A (all had to go because mom was working late)
Tuesday: soccer practice B and Cub Scouts (divide and conquer)
Wednesday: piano lessons
Thursday: home
Friday: team A scheduled another practice
Saturday: games for teams A and B
Sunday: church in a.m. and choir in p.m.

It just became too much for us. So, we decided that church was vital to our weekly rhythm. After that, the boys could do one extra thing. This was not an easy decision. At the time, I felt that I was letting down our kids, and our teams. I even thought that I could be affecting our children's future. They were six and eight. Here is what we had to ask ourselves: Are the kids happy or not?

I wrote the following blog in 2012 about being overscheduled and how I felt about it. I think it was a great perspective as I now look back on pieces of my parenting journey:

> We all know that when I can put something into an Excel spreadsheet or into my Google calendar, it makes me happy. But scheduling a family can be a nightmare when you have more than one activity going on.
>
> This year Slick is in baseball and Scouts. Mr. D is also in baseball and Scouts.
>
> Now, I did not even mention PTA, playdates, night meetings at work, make-up games, batting practice, study groups, Mr. stuck in traffic, one kid sick, one parent sick, and the fact that they both want to do tae kwon do. Practices, Scout meetings, and games rule our lives. Oh, wait, don't forget that I am in grad school, and Dan commutes 45 minutes each way every day. I will say that sharing a Google calendar with Mr. D on our phones sure does help with the "who goes where when" thing!
>
> I am lucky enough to have a work schedule that means I am home when my kids get out of school. We do snacks and chill for a bit when they get home, and then do homework and any chores. It is hard sometimes to keep school and homework first. But I have to remind myself (and my boys) that school is their job

now. It should always come first. That does not mean that it always does, but it is our goal.

I have clipboards, so if we are at a practice, the other kiddo can work on homework. It is not ideal, but it gets it done.

So, this is how it goes:

Monday: we don't have a practice or anything (breathe)
Tuesday: baseball and Scouts
Wednesday: Scouts (and several games this night)
Thursday: baseball
Saturday: games / Scout activities / church outreach events

I am in class on Wednesday, so between Mr. D., my parents, and my dear friends, people get where they need to go.

We get a rhythm going. I go here, and Mr. D goes there. It is fine. It works.

This is our last weekend of baseball. This gives me joy! I love watching my boys play, but I will also love not having practices and games for a while.

I tried to talk both of my boys out of Scouts this year. But they love it. (It is not that I don't—I was trying to have a slower routine for the week.)

This I how I deal when it gets to be too much, too fast, too late. We don't go. We stay home, and it is OK. The games go on without us. The meetings go on without us. Now, I don't do this too often. We did commit, and it is important to live up to our commitments. But it is also important to slow down sometimes. To sit and be.

Honoring Your Child's Hopes and Dreams

Throughout my life, I have had the opportunity to be a part of so many different family's lives, as a teacher, a director of a preschool, a children's pastor, a family pastor, a PTA mom, and a football mom. The parents that have always piqued my interest are the ones who know who their child is and embrace it. Let's be honest. As parents, we have hopes and dreams for our children that can differ from what their own interests are.

One of the hardest things I had to do was to let go of my dreams for my kids, to let go of who I thought my kids were. They have never disappointed me in being who they are. In fact, the opposite. They impress me tremendously. Allowing them to grow and merge fully into whom they were created to be can be challenging for parents, but the rewards are so much greater. You give your children your ultimate respect when you honor who they are and the goals they set for themselves.

I am not a sports person. I have never really paid much attention to any sport, professional or college. It's just not my thing. I like to say that I don't have any more emotional energy to put into another bucket in my life. Well, that has changed, because my boys have changed me. They love sports. Growing up, they played for a team (typically baseball), took piano, and were in the church choir. In middle school, they were both in the band. Our oldest did band his freshman year and quickly realized that this was not for him. It was a very long year. This was the same year that both sons let me know that choir was something they were doing for others (myself, my mom, and the directors) but that they no longer enjoyed it. Allowing them to walk away from this broke my heart. This meant no more leading in worship, no more choir tours. It was hard for my boys to tell me this, but it was honest and real. I am glad that our youngest has still found a way to express himself with music through guitar and working with the youth worship choir. Our oldest does not express himself with music. But he writes, he reads, he is him. As you are reading this, you might think, no big deal, they are not in the church choir. You are correct. This was not a huge life decision, but yet, I had to let go of a dream that I had, a dream that was mine and not theirs. Instead, I had to embrace what they are passionate about: high school football.

As I am writing this, I volunteer for the football team as a varsity team mom. I go to all the games. I support them, and I love watching them. I know the difference between offense and defense, and I am learning the rules and penalties.

I learned to love it. My boys have such a passion and dedication to getting healthier, to learning about the different plays. They work out before school, after school, and on the weekend. I not only love this sport but also see it as a gift to me. I grew up with some preconceived notions of what sports were, mostly high school football in Texas. Yet, I have learned some critical lessons about my assumptions because of my kids.

The family that I have now loves sports. All sports. And I am learning. I am learning the language, the attitude, the different plays, the different uniforms, and all the other rules.

The year my oldest was on a newly formed baseball team, it took a few games to win one. They have good players and good coaches, yet they had not developed a rhythm as a team. It's hard to go out every game and lose. It's hard to keep your spirits up. It's hard to keep trying. I thought, "Well, this has been a great lesson on losing."

At the end of each game, the coaches would discuss the

different mistakes (which I now know are called errors) and the plays that were well executed. Then the coach would say, "I am proud of you, boys." I am ashamed to say after a challenging game when the coach said, "I am proud of you, boys," I thought, "No, stop saying that! Tell them they must work harder, they must communicate as a team, they must . . . ." Then I knew I was wrong.

The losing wasn't the point. The playing was the point. After one game, we received an email from the coach listing every player and why he was proud of their playing. He then told them to keep working and practicing all week long and to remember that the next game will be a brand-new opportunity to play.

My perspective on dreams?

- Keep your eyes on what is happening now. It is messy, and it is beautiful. This is your family.
- Lean into your kids' passions, especially if they are different from yours.
- Learn from them.
- Revel in who they are. The moments pass by so fast, and every day is a blessing.
- Take a deep breath and smile.

The points above are simple words put into simple sentences but living out these points is very difficult. When you have had a bad day and the house is a mess, your child went to bed crying, you still have a deadline at work, and it just seems like it's too much, this is when you need perspective the most. This book is to remind you that you can do hard things. Learning from our children helps us become better people, not just better parents.

Parenting Perspective: Carolyn Getridge
Parent, Grandparent, Retired School Superintendent

From the moment you hear the words, "You're going to have a baby," your dreams and expectations for your life are forever altered. You have vivid images of all their milestones—the birth, first steps and words, and their first day of kindergarten—and before you know it, high school prom and graduation are here. Most often the reality of parenting paints a very different picture than that which you imagined. Life does not unfold in the carefully organized and timely manner that you have envisioned. It just happens. As a parent and a lifelong educator, I have learned to seek joy in each moment.

Love unconditionally and appreciate the uniqueness of the gift that you have been given. Yours is the opportunity to nurture and develop the talents and skills that are distinct to this individual. Even within the same family, both the gifts and the approaches will differ. Allow your children to explore various interests to discover their talents and passions. Resist the temptation to compare your children with others. Focus on discerning and cultivating your children's gifts and support them in realizing their full potential. Cherish the successes and embrace the moments—both large and small.

Accept the challenges and learn from them. As difficult as the situation may be, know that this is not the end. As a middle school principal, I often spent as much time counseling and supporting parents as I did students. Adolescence is tough, and the physical and emotional imbalances that are more pronounced during this period can be overwhelming for parents and children. Take the time, without judgment, to ask the critical questions: What did you do? Why did you do it? If you could have made a different choice, what would you have done? What have you learned from this experience? Though often distressful, these lessons will be treasured as your children grow.

Instill values and beliefs not only with your words but also through your actions. You are your children's first teachers. They see and hear you. As they grow, they learn who you are and what you value. Live the Golden Rule: do unto others as you would have them do unto you. Show compassion and empathy. Be patient, honest, and respectful. See the good in others, and seek to find the good in every experience. Each day demonstrate the traits and behaviors that you want your children to develop. As they grow, these behaviors will define their character and bring happiness to them and to others.

Throughout my life, I have held the same aspirations for other people's children as I have for my own. Each life is a gift and has purpose. I have been inspired and guided by the words of Jeremiah 29:11, "For I know the plans I have for you," declares the LORD, "plans to prosper you and not to harm you, plans to give you hope and a future" (NIV). I believe that God's plans are perfect, and I count it all joy.

Dear God who has created our most precious gifts,

I thank you for the person you've placed in our family's midst. I know each smile, each sigh, each freckle and dimple. And sometimes I even think I know what their day might hold. And then something changes, something grows, something shifts, and our world shakes.

I know this child intimately, and yet, she (he) is also a mystery known only to you. I pray for your vision—to look upon this child with your eyes and heart. She (He) is whole, right now. She (He) is enough, right now. She (He) is a glimpse of your kingdom, right now.

May I find the strength to let go of my desires and instead take up your hope—that she (he) would know your love and show your love to everyone she (he) meets, just the way you created her (him) to do.

And as for me, God, I pray for self-compassion as I journey through the new creation you are doing in me. I look to You, who have parented me with grace and freedom, as a guide to shaping the life you entrusted to me. Our family is coming together, God. I pray that I might grow toward You in the midst.

In your Son Jesus Christ's name I pray, amen.

Rev. Emma Williams

9 You Will Love Them So Much It Hurts

If I speak in the tongues of mortals and of angels, but do not have love, I am a noisy gong or a clanging cymbal. And if I have prophetic powers, and understand all mysteries and all knowledge, and if I have all faith, so as to remove mountains, but do not have love, I am nothing. If I give away all my possessions, and if I hand over my body so that I may boast, but do not have love, I gain nothing.

Love is patient; love is kind; love is not envious or boastful or arrogant or rude. It does not insist on its own way; it is not irritable or resentful; it does not rejoice in wrongdoing, but rejoices in the truth. It bears all things, believes all things, hopes all things, endures all things.

Love never ends. But as for prophecies, they will come to an end; as for tongues, they will cease; as for knowledge, it will come to an end. For we know only in part, and we prophesy only in part; but when the complete comes, the partial will come to an end. When I was a child, I spoke like a child, I thought like a child, I reasoned like a child; when I became an adult, I put an end to childish ways. For now we see in a mirror, dimly, but then we will see face to face. Now I know only in part; then I will know fully, even as I have been fully known. And now faith, hope, and love abide, these three; and the greatest of these is love.

1 Corinthians 13

This scripture reminds us what love is and what love can be. Humble and gentle, patient, and bearing with one another in love. *Bearing*, this is not a word that we use often. It is defined as the act of enduring or having the capacity to endure. Love is a privilege. God has first loved us, and it is in that love that we find the example of what love can be.

These verses are so straightforward, but simplicity has great depth and power. I pray that you will use this passage as more than words in a book but as the living word of God. In your actions with one another, try to live out of these descriptors:

Humble
Gentle
Patient
Kind
Tenderhearted
Forgiving
In my love . . .

When you need support the most, lean into the example that God has given us for how to love one another.

A Parent's Love

That baby . . . how can you love someone so much who is so new to your life? Every parent gets such a feeling of intense love and pride when they welcome that new addition to their family. I could not believe how much love I had for this little person who entered my life. As a mom, this child has forever changed my body but also my heart and soul. As a father, your connection between world and self is forever altered. I think there is a connection between parent and child that has no proper description, except exquisite love.

Family life can be much harder than anticipated. Family has so many different emotions and people in it. I love having kids and most that comes with it, but some days are harder than others. When you need a perspective switch, think about this question: What do you love about having kids?

Here are some fun parts of parenting:

- The smiles, especially when picking them up from school or an event.
- The family snuggles / movie nights.
- Hugs—there is just something about hugging your child, even better is receiving a hug from your kids.
- The love—a love between parent and child is like no other love.
- Being able to watch them grow and become independent.
- Learning new things together.
- Traditions, both old and new, that will be forever a part of your family.
- Generations—connecting the family from child to grand parents, aunts, cousins. This bond is so powerful.

When They Hurt, and You Can't Fix It

I genuinely believe that the most challenging part of being a parent is when your kids hurt (both physically and emotionally), and you can't fix it for them. I remember when our infant son needed breathing treatments every four hours. This was not a physically painful thing, but the breathing mask over his face just made him scream. We got through it and found ways to distract him, but at the time, his infant cries made me wish I could fix his little lungs, and I just could not.

When you know your child is suffering (physically or emotionally), most of the time, you have zero ability to fix it. You can't take away the pain of an injury, their first friend fight or drama, their first breakup, or the diagnosis at the doctor's office that you can't believe is your child's. There are so many things that can break when it comes to our humanity. There are so many examples of how your child can hurt, and you can't fix any of it for them.

I recently had a great conversation with our son about a breakup and a change among some of his friends. This process was painful to watch as a parent. I wanted to swoop in and fix everything for him. I am so grateful that my kids' first breakups happened when they were under our roof. I could not stop the sadness and hurt that comes with a broken heart. But I could listen, surround them with unconditional love, ask if they wanted to talk, and of course, provide all the ice cream.

So many things can cause pain to our kids, and yet we keep sending them out the door. Why? Because putting them in a bubble in their rooms will not teach them how to heal or grow as a human. When there is brokenness, there must also be healing. Healing can be painful, but typically we learn so much in the process.

As parents we want so many things for our children, but ultimately it boils down to two primary things:

1) Love God fully.
2) Love others fully.

This is why I say this to them as often as I can:

1) Don't be stupid. (When they were younger, this rule was titled "Make good choices.")
2) Remember whose you are.

If they can follow these two rules, it can help them center decisions ultimately in loving God and loving others.

I am not naive enough to think that if you follow these simple rules, nothing will be painful. But I do believe they can help us reset what is important. They can help me understand that I can't control the universe, the kids at school, or the pain of an injury. But I can show deep and true unconditional love. I can control how I love.

Grace for You

I will always love you; I might not always like you. This is something that I first heard from my mom. She would say it in many ways, but the same theme was still valid. She would always love me, but some days it was hard to like me. I don't think I fully understood this until one of our children shouted during a consequence, "I hate you." Gasp! How could you hate me? I do so much for you. I love you so much. My son came out of his room with an attitude that pushed all my buttons. At this moment, I fully understood that there are days when we may not like our kids. That is OK.

It is not OK to stay in that place. But it is OK to feel it. Give yourself grace and some time to heal. Love is hard. Parenting is harder.

I have a vivid memory of reading the comics with my dad on Sunday mornings. I had some favorites, but a strong memory is the "Love is" comics by Kim Casali.

I loved this comic because it gave life to what love is. Now, as a parent, it gives me a whole new perspective. I have the burden of seeing life as an adult, not as a child. I see the bad and the good, then toss in my education in theology, and it adds a whole new perspective. So, I ask you, What is love? I believe that love is in relationships, in each relationship. It is not a one-size-fits-all glove.

I love me some Jesus.
I love my parents and family.
I love my husband.
I love my children.

I love my friends.

I love the churches I serve.

I like sushi.

I like a good glass of red wine on a winter night.

I like a good book.

I like a long walk.

When we look at the word *love* as a verb and not a noun, we can change how we choose to love.

I think that sometimes we forget about what love is. It is not some movie screen or commercial ad. It is real, and real life gets messy. It is full of emotions that I would rather have than not, but at times they are muddy. Love is constant. Love is true. Love is something that we all aspire to do and, at times, fall short of. This is what I know and believe: I love God. I love the people in my life. I love my family. I love my friends. Each love is different, but each love is real. That does not mean that I like each family member or my friends every day, but the love holds fast. At the beginning of this chapter I quoted 1 Corinthians 13. This Bible verse is used at many weddings that I officiate. I always tell the couple that love is a four-letter word. It is not easy. This hits me because sometimes, in my "love," I am angry, envious, arrogant, and rude. But, because of the love inside me, I can calm down and know and remember that the relationship is still grounded in love.

Parenting Perspective: Kelly Hoxsey
Parent, Counselor

Parenting intentionally out of love is God's call to all parents as it is in every other relationship. Don't parent out of anger, frustration, intolerance, or even hunger. Love. Just love. Love your child as you tell them to bring their personal items from the bottom of the stairs into their bedroom for the tenth time? Yep. Love them as your kids fuss with their siblings over whose turn it is? Yep. Love them in return of their snarly teenage attitude? Yep, even then too.

Jesus calls us all to do what I refer to as using superhuman strength. He wants his followers to be more like Him, more like the loving parent that He is to all of us. Regardless of the words we use, the tone we have, and the poor decisions that we make, we are the blessed recipients of God's unconditional love. Sitting quietly and resting in that is both comforting and perplexing.

I cannot imagine all of the misaligned thoughts, feelings, and actions from the fruits of the spirit that God has witnessed His children making. Still, He loves us all unconditionally. As I work with parents, I ask them to choose a word or phrase that will help remind them to be responsive instead of reactive. This quick pause to choose how to respond gives them a chance to conjure the superhuman strength that comes from the Holy Spirit. I offer examples to respond through the filter of kindness, patience, and respect; however, when I add the example of responding in the same way that we worship God, it all clicks. Leveling up to the path Jesus wants us to follow not only holds us to a higher form of care but also simplifies the path, as it is clear what we must choose. On my best days, I personally use the phrase, "How can I handle this in a way that glorifies God?" (usually as I take deep breaths in my closet). On my worst days, I regret not being intentional to use that filter in my response. I appreciate Eugene Peterson's interpretation of 1 Corinthians 10: "No test or temptation that comes your way is beyond the course of what others have had to face. All you need to remember is that God will never let you down; he'll never let you be pushed past your limit; he'll always be there to help you come through it" (v. 13 MSG). This helps reassure me that when I rely on God to help guide me through a challenging situation, He will be right there waiting to guide me through it in a loving way.

I've often heard women speaking of "mom guilt" as the worst guilt they experience, and I can well relate to that feeling. Just as the mistakes we make can cut deeply into our children's hearts, they also cut into our own. I occasionally meet someone who does not apologize to others. These people have a path of relationships damaged by pride and self-righteousness, and when they have an open heart and mind, they typically find apologizing not only to be easier than expected but also much more helpful than they were prepared for. The willingness to model a healing apology to our children demonstrates how to take responsibility and offer amends that can not only heal your relationship with your child but also prepare him or her for a life full of apologies and the knowledge of how to recover from the regrettable decisions we make. Here's an example of a recent apology I gave to one of my kids: "I'm sorry for rushing you and being short-tempered. It was wrong because you were doing the best you could, and

I made the stress worse by rushing you with reminders. Next time I will give you the space to do what you need to do without me nagging you. Will you forgive me?" This four-step approach (apologizing, explaining why what you did was wrong, what you are apologizing for, and what you will do differently next time) has proven to be effective to take responsibility and make amends. My family offers grace for mistakes, and hard as it may be to give at times, it's certainly appreciated when it's me on the receiving end of that grace.

Another offer of love for our children is to love them as God created them to be, not how we want them, planned for them, prepared them, engineered them, or begged them to be. The phrase "Grieve the loss of the child you wished you had and fall in love with the one you do have" is a powerful phrase and an even much more powerful experience. We all want to be recognized and appreciated for who we are and not who others wish we were. This applies to a child who is interested in science or music, but his dad really wants to coach him in sports. Or simply a parent who wants her child to fulfill his God-given potential but her child prefers a different path. I can authentically share that regulating my tone or words when I'm frustrated with my own children is a piece of cake compared to honoring who my child believes God has called them to be instead of my own design for their lives. After all, God created us all in His image, and we are His masterpiece. We trust in Him by loving the way He created our children. We glorify God in the way we love His creation.

Lord,

thank you for this amazing child. I love her (him)
more than I thought was possible. I ask that you will always
be in her (his) heart. When she (he) is feeling loved
or lost, broken or whole, humble or boastful; stay in her (his) heart
and show her (him) that you are in everything she (he) sees
and does. I ask that you cover her (him) in your protection, both
physically and emotionally, and that your goodness proves
to be more powerful.

In your name I pray, amen.

Amy O'Hare

10   You Will Have Days When You Don't Like Who They Are

Have you not known? Have you not heard?
The LORD is the everlasting God,
the Creator of the ends of the earth.
He does not faint or grow weary;
his understanding is unsearchable.
He gives power to the faint,
and strengthens the powerless.
Even youths will faint and be weary,
and the young will fall exhausted;
but those who wait for the LORD shall renew their strength,
they shall mount up with wings like eagles,
they shall run and not be weary,
they shall walk and not faint.

Isaiah 40:28-31

It's Complicated

Some days, as a parent, you won't like who your children are, even though you will still love them to the moon and back. A relationship between parent and child is complicated. This is not some TV show where in thirty minutes you have a problem and solution. This is your family. You see them every day. These are the people who know you the best, which means that they are also the people who can push your buttons like no others. Your parent-child relationship is unlike any other partnership that you have ever had. In a marriage partnership, you are equal with each other. You might have different gifts that you bring into the relationship, but you share a true and equal partnership. In parenting, you are the parent, and your child is the child. This never changes. It develops, grows, and matures. But it never really changes.

As the parent, you will set some rules and boundaries that your child will not like, and they could be quite mean about it. I did this with my parents. I was a very strong-willed and outspoken child. I am sure my parents had many moments when they went into another room and had to count to ten before responding to one of my outbursts. On the other hand, my sister was very passive when it came to responding to my parents. Here is an example:

> *My Parents:* "Kim and Erin, we need you to clean your rooms by 3:00 today."
> *Kim:* "I am swamped today. I can't believe that you are being so oppressive and demanding that I pick up my room. Next time I would appreciate some more time to clean. You never listen to me!" She slams door. Then cleans the room.
> *Erin:* "OK." She would then proceed to go into her room and read books and not clean anything.

Same parents, same house, two very different children. This is hard.

I will never forget when I started at a new church, and I was meeting different people. My introductions were the same most of the time: "We have two children who are in first and third grade," I said. One wise person paused, and with a smile on his face, responded with, "Oh, so they are not assholes yet." I was a bit taken aback by this sentence. Yet, he was right. Now that I have two high school students, I get it.

We have had some long and loud nights at our house parenting. Sometimes we were up with a crying infant. Sometimes we were battling bedtime, turning off the Wi-Fi, or questioning how we might be screwing up our kids. But, in these moments of tension, grace and love have always won.

It does not always feel like that in the tension, but after I snapped, or my child snapped, there was always a moment of love and forgiveness. This is what has made our family stronger, wiser, and more connected.

The hardest part of my life is letting go of control. To give control to God is the hardest and the most freeing thing for me in any aspect of my life. I know that I am here to live out the best life I can in honor of God. So, the feeling that I get in letting go of my need for control to a God who gives me grace and peace in times of change is strangely peaceful. I think of Matthew 8:26: "[Jesus] replied, "You of little faith, why are you so afraid?" Then he got up and rebuked the winds and the waves, and it was completely calm" (NIV). I feel this kind of peace in my moments of release. Then I breathe and try again to regain my control. It is a constant process for me. This is similar to a teenager who is learning how to drive. Remember learning how to apply the brake smoothly? Remember the first time in the car when you need to slow down, and you slammed on the brake? You eventually learned that this hurts! Applying pressure slowly is a better way to use the brakes, and a better way to handle a need for control. When we let too much control build up, the breakthrough hurts. We must remember that slowly, throughout the day, each and every day, we must let go and give our lives to God. This is the peaceful way to live out our faith, and our role as a parent.

Nothing can separate my children and my love for them. There may be times where I'm not too fond of their actions, their decisions, or even them. But love can help us heal and come back together.

When Kids Mess Up

What happens when your kids mess up, and you are shocked at what they did?

No matter the mistake, if you are shocked by the behavior, it is probably because they acted the opposite of the morals, values, and ethics you felt you instilled in your children.

What do we do with this?

My first response is typically anger, shame, and guilt, all rolled into one giant emotion that, for me, naturally comes with loud words and tears.

This is where I will be forever grateful that my partner in this parenting gig is a very calm soul. So, my next healthy response is typically asking myself if I ever made mistakes as a child or teenager? I like to try to gain some perspective, because I desperately need to understand why my child made such a poor decision. Sometimes the answer is simple: they made a mistake, a poor choice. They responded to a situation in a reactive way, not in a responsible manner.

This does not make them horrible humans; it also does not make you awful parents. It means that mistakes were made. We can keep mistakes in a cycle of drama, or we can find opportunities to grow.

When a child does something wrong it can easily become a vicious circle. The wrong action is followed by a reaction from the parent or other adult – either of frustration or anger. The child responds to that reaction in a way that depends on how they see authority figures, but it leads to a negative view of themselves, which makes them more likely to do wrong again. And then, rinse and repeat!!! (I've adapted this from the work by Charles Fay, the founder of Love and Logic parenting books. Charles Fay, "The Misbehavior Cycle," Love and Logic, https://www.loveandlogic.com/pages/misbehavior-cycle).

We can stop this cycle (we can't stop the mistakes) by walking the different mistakes along with our children, showing the consequences of their actions or allowing the natural consequences to happen, and moving on. It is important for me to highlight the "moving on" part. When mistakes happen, nobody likes to be constantly reminded of that. This is the same in our children. As parents it is important for us to move forward after a mistake, this allows our children to also move forward.

This is an opportunity to show the love and grace we talked about so much. Now, showing love and grace does not mean that you don't have consequences for their actions. There are always consequences for our actions. But it is showing them that they don't have to walk this journey alone. That even if they disappoint you, your love is more significant than that.

Our kids will disappoint us. They will embarrass us. Our family uses humor in most life situations, even if it is not entirely appropriate. That is a fair warning for this next section. If our kids are driving us crazy, we have the expression, "Ugh, children." When we are driving them crazy, they will say, "Ugh, parents." This seems very simple, but it brings a bit of comic relief when we might be frustrated with one another. It helps us understand that having kids is hard, and being a parent is hard. It also helps us know that growing up, too, is hard.

So, when mistakes are made that you don't even want to tell your best friend about, remind yourself that mistakes are a part of life, that we can do hard things and still find a way to learn and move on.

You Are Blessed to Be a Blessing

I am a true believer that children are connected to the spiritual world. I truly believe that children have a natural connection to God and creation (nature). One way to put it is that children have a connection to a higher power. One of my good friends reminded me of this, pointing out how their children's relationship with nature is full of curiosity and wonderment. I can remember finding as many roly-polies as I could find. I watched them crawl around and then, in a second, stop and roll into a ball of safety. How is this connected to God? Great question. The wonderment of our natural world is that we have a connection between ourselves and something greater. As children are asking questions: Why is the sky blue? Where did the bird learn to build a nest? How is a rainbow made? These questions help them create connections between creation and our creator.

We see the simple connection between children and God when it comes to prayer. I have been in many different meetings and conferences, where when adults are asked to pray, they will all look down and say a silent prayer, so that they will become invisible. I have also been in a Sunday morning small group with our elementary-age children. When I ask a child to pray, five hands go up as they pray for birthday parties, goldfish, football games, grandparents, new shoes, and sleepovers. They pray for everything they can. What happens between the age of eight and thirty-eight?

I think we make prayer bigger than it is. Prayer is simply a time to connect to God, who wants to be in a relationship with us.

Prayer does not have to be silent reverence with candles and music. But, it can be.

Prayer does not have to be a liturgy that comes from tradition. But, it can be.

Prayer does not have to be bowing of head and folding of hands. But, it can be.

Prayer can be what you want it to be, simple or scripted.

Prayer as a family can help connect us to one another and to God. Telling our faith's stories (I am taking a Christian perspective, because I am a Christian pastor) helps our children know that they are, first and foremost, a child of God. Why is this important? In our family, prayer connects our children to God (Father/Creator, Son, and Holy Spirit) and the stories of our faith. We believe these stories are God's living word, which can mean that we are a part of the story. We teach our children that their identity is grounded in being made perfect in the image of God. This is profound. And it is powerful.

It is also true. A dear friend of mine, Rev. Dr. Leanne Hadley, taught me about giving children blessings. It is a simple practice where you can use your finger or some "blessing balm" (typically ChapStick) and say, "You are blessed to be a blessing." The first time you do it, you feel the difference in the room. When you stop and pause, remind children that they are a blessing created to bless others. This communicates to them from a young age that they are loved fully for who they are, with all their quirks and all their talents. They are assured that they can help make this world a better place. The real moment of transformation is when a child then, in return, asks if they can bless you. Especially if this is your child. Having your child take the lead in faith development, grab your hand, look you in the eyes, and say, "You are blessed to be a blessing" changes you. We all need to be told we are a blessing and that we can be a blessing to others.

Let me tell you simply how instilling this in our children has changed their lives. When you don't make the team, your girlfriend/boyfriend breaks up with you, you fail a test, or you don't get the job/promotion, your child will recognize that as a disappointment. They may be sad. The experience is painful, but their disappointment does not describe who they are. Their most important definition is, I am a child of God. This is powerful and true. This knowledge can bring great perspective on disappointment in your life and your child's. I am speaking from experience on this one. This can save lives and can transform bad days into beautiful ones.

My dear reader, you are blessed to be a blessing. I don't even know you, but I believe that fully.

Parenting Perspective: Deborah Walsh Dobbs
Parent, Victim Advocate

I hadn't planned on being a parent, and I had my reasons. For starters, I loved my job. I was a victim advocate and on-call almost every night. It wasn't a schedule conducive to parenting, and the constant exposure to trauma and all-around suffering drained me physically and emotionally. I was selfish with my time off, which came in short bursts. I wanted to travel, sleep late on the weekends, be spontaneous, and take hot baths whenever and for however long I desired. I'll also go ahead and admit it: I wasn't all that crazy about kids. I tried to avoid them as much as possible.

The Alpha and Omega had other plans for me, though, and at age thirty-five, I found myself pregnant. Fortunately for me (and my daughter), I had lots of support. The job that drained me of all my energy also surrounded me with mental health professionals who worked with kids, teens, and parents and were experts in child development. My social circle was small but mighty. A few of my friends had already secured their footing in parenthood, and they were merely a phone call away. My parents offered time, energy, and guidance for my motherhood journey, and they lived less than ten minutes from me.

I vowed to be the best parent I could possibly be. It helped that my mom and dad had provided a good parenting model. Like most of us, I selected techniques they implemented in their parenting style and opted out of others. Among the many keepers: the way they exposed me to other cultures, how they valued education without being snobby about it, and never pushed me into gender roles. What didn't make the cut was yelling. My mom could be a yeller, but I wasn't going to yell at my child. Ever.

My marriage ended before my kiddo completed preschool. Despite that, she seemed like a happy child. She was extraordinarily healthy and strong. She was a cuddler yet incredibly brave. She learned to swim when she was a baby. By the time she was eighteen months old, she could jump into the deep end of the pool and swim to the edge and get out without assistance. She loved the music of Johnny Cash and Ruthie Foster. She was a food adventurer, who was helping me cook when she was still in diapers. She was kindhearted, generous, and unnervingly intuitive. Her preschool teachers referred to her as "little Jesus." At a very young age, she showed an astounding amount of empathy and a love for God. She also displayed near impeccable table manners, and other adults consistently remarked on how polite she was. Granted, she had her moments and pushed boundaries. (The swim teacher, after all, implored me to read *The Strong-Willed Child* by Dr. James Dobson.) Overall, though, and with seemingly little effort on my part, my baby evolved into a loving, intelligent young girl, who was often described as beautiful inside and out.

Wherever there is beauty, predators appear. The predator was middle school.

My daughter was always her own person, with interests and preferences unlike mine. She was never my "mini me," but once middle school inserted itself into our lives, she seemed to hold me in utter contempt. Daily, I braced myself for who would emerge from her lair in the morning or come through the front door in the afternoon. I loved her, and I proved that every day. But I didn't like her all that much anymore. I often felt angered by her, and I remember yelling so loudly I thought I'd channeled Sam Kinison. (*I wasn't going to yell.* Who was I kidding?) As the leader of a mental health agency, surrounded by experts, I thought I should be doing better. At times I felt like a failure.

One morning, as I stood outside her bedroom door, checking my emotional armor before entering, I reflected on my own adolescence. I bet I wasn't incredibly likeable when I was a teen in the '80s. How much more unlikeable would I have been as a teen with divorced parents whose households functioned like two different planets? How would I have managed with an undeveloped brain in this instant gratification, constant stimulation society? How might I have fared in a culture where "normal" isn't cool or even acceptable, where for many it's not enough to be liked by some of their peers, but they must have the approval of thousands of strangers too? Every mistake can be recorded, edited, and broadcast throughout the world within seconds. I probably would've been a basket case, and sadly, many teens these days are.

The contrast between our cultures and experiences allowed me to reframe the situation. I did like her. What I didn't like was her behavior. I didn't like the way she was responding to her environment, which included me. And if I told myself I didn't like *her,* she would certainly feel that. I mean, most of us have been around someone who didn't like us, and you didn't have to be an empath to detect it. She also undoubtedly felt my anger, and that wasn't going to alleviate any tension. I also had to wonder if I was mirroring her, or if she was mirroring me. (We likely took turns, depending on the day.) As for my anger, it's rarely a standalone emotion, and I realized mine was guarding my grief and fear. I *missed* my daughter, and I was worried about her. That was behind my anger. What was behind hers?

I also considered that the girl on the other side of that door was the same girl who, a decade earlier, taught me to take in the good, stop rushing, and pay attention to the small stuff—turns out the small stuff is some of the best stuff and absolutely worthy of sweat. Before the girl could speak, she encouraged me to be fully present and grateful for the little things, to explore my surroundings, to observe butterflies, to stop cursing dandelions in our yard, and to discover beauty in odd places, like in the cracks in the sidewalk. The moody girl who was taking to extremes the development of an identity separate from me was the same girl who taught me some invaluable lessons that brought joy back to my life. She was a blessing then, and she was a blessing still. Maybe a blessing wearing porcupine skin several days a week, but nonetheless a blessing.

The clarity provided by my reframing the big picture didn't transform our relationship into a Hallmark movie ending. We rock-and-rolled and still do. (At the time of this writing, she's only fifteen, so we have a ways to go.) I yell, but not nearly as often. The frame tends to fall from the big picture and often needs replacing, yet when I do it, we get through the harder days with less gnashing of teeth. It helps me take a breath, not the bait. During these rough spots, I reassure myself (and sometimes my daughter) that the teen years are difficult, but they're also temporary, even though sometimes it feels like they're passing at a snail's pace. My daughter is in high school now, and she and I laugh more, like we used to. She talks to me again, not about everything (that would be weird), but at least she's talking.

I hadn't planned on being a parent, but I'm a better human for doing it. I've learned how to love fully, even when I don't love a person's behavior, even when the person isn't great at loving me back or even recoils from my effort. Parenthood has incorporated in me a different dimension of compassion for others. It has tested my sanity and revealed that I'm tougher than I thought. It has cultivated wisdom I never thought I'd had. While I still don't always like my daughter's behavior, eye rolls, sighs, or blank expressions she gives in response to the simplest request, I do indeed like *her* as a human, as a blessing.

Dear Gracious and Loving God,

From the moment I saw my children, I had this overwhelming knowledge that I was responsible to love and care for them. But how? Through the moments and years, I have come to rely on the love that you have for your children as an example of how to love my children. The patience, the kindness, the pride, the heartache. It all goes together.

Help me to love them without smothering, to support them without being a crutch, and to correct without breaking their spirit. When I fall or stumble at the task before me, help me get back up and continue to love as you have loved.

Guard my heart, give me strength, give me the words, and celebrate the small moments of parenthood.

In your precious and loving name, I pray, amen.

Kristen Lane

11   You Will Need a Village

Two are better than one, because they have a good reward
for their toil.

Ephesians 2:10

Who is Your Partner?

Earlier in the book I talked about a white water rafting trip. The guide gave us instructions, then let us practice on some smaller rapids. But then the guide did something that has stuck with me. After every rapid that we crossed, he had us turn around and look at what we had come through. "That was a class 2, next is a class 3, get ready," he would say. Each time while we were in calm waters, he would have us turn around and see the rapids that we accomplished together. This has changed me, how I look upon my life, and how I do life with others. It has affirmed the connection that we have with creation.

Some of us live in a class 4 rapid. We are working hard to move and get through, and we can't see much else. Some of us live in class 3. It takes work and focus, but we can do this. Some of us live in class 2. It has some bumps and some waves, but it is smooth all in all. But no matter what kind of life we are living, we all need people in the boat with us. We all need instructors guiding us. And we need to look at the past and be able also to see the present and the future. This is done best when you are in a community, especially a community of faith.

We are not meant to do life alone; I think that is even more true for parenting. At the current church I serve, we have a podcast called "Lift." The introduction to each episode is:

> Welcome to *Lift: A Parenting Podcast,* where we ask
> questions about family and faith. Parenting takes a lot
> of heavy lifting, in physical, emotional, and spiritual
> ways. Let's face it: raising a family is hard work. Some
> of us are doing it as a single parent; some of us are
> working with a spouse, but all of us have questions ev-
> ery day. Are we screwing up our kids? Our marriage?
> Our relationships? This podcast will ask questions
> that can guide each of us to finding our rhythm and
> creating space for God in our home.

I genuinely believe that we seek one another's wisdom and
support to be the best parents we can be. Before I go any further in this section, let me say that I do not understand what
it's like to be a single parent or work with an ex-spouse as a
co-parent. I honor and respect those of you who do this. But
I want to say that, even if this is the case, everyone needs a
go-to, a partner who can pick us up when we need it the most.

So, who is your partner? If I answer this question, my
number one is my husband, Dan. We work hard together to
parent our kids. But if I am honest, we have many other partners who help Dan and me do this great task. We have friends,
family, pastors, counselors, teachers, neighbors, and coaches.
They all have helped to speak into our lives and our children's
lives in real and valuable ways.

When I was growing up, I babysat almost every weekend
for a family at our church. Their home became a second home
to me. This family had become partners with my parents and
with me. In fact, without me knowing, if my parents were
struggling with me on a subject or wondering about something in my life, they would call this other family and ask the

parents to connect with me on every subject. I would typically open up to them in ways that I would not with my parents. I applaud my parents for this method. This is what community does for one another—they lean on one another when they can't do it alone.

I don't know what I would do without the many people who help us. I am truly grateful for the community that helps me raise my kids.

Real Friends

I am a person who loves to be around people. This gives me energy, love, and support. This does not mean that I would tell all people all things. This is reserved for a very small few. I am fortunate that I have surrounded myself with loving and deep friendships throughout my life. I still talk almost daily with a group of women from college. I have several adult friends who know what I think before I say it. I have a group of pastors who are my place to go when I need a safe place.

I believe that each group of loyal friends that I have help me be a better person. They call me out when I am not myself. They let me cry when that is all I need to do. They listen to my thoughts and fears that are so hard to admit to. They give me a safe space. I don't know how I would do it without this support group. We love one another's kids with a deep, true love. Some of these children don't know who we are, but we know and love them fully. The more adults who can truly love and pray for my kids, the better!

I love my husband—deeply, truly, love him. He is my guy. But sometimes, I need to vent, talk to another mom or wife, and have a village of people who get it in a way my husband just can't. Here is a bit of a warning. Dan still needs to be my number one. There was a period where I found myself going to my girlfriends for 90 percent of my problems and ended leaving Dan on the outside of some of my thoughts. That was not good. I have found a better balance between leaning on Dan as my number one supporter and leaning on my friends to support me too.

When you find your people, keep them close. One of my deepest friends has coined a little statement that we text back and forth to each other: "We could be in Hawaii." Let me explain. This friend at one time was also my neighbor, a couple (without kids) who lived near us.

They had the fancy cars. We picked up their mail when they went on fancy trips. We also asked ourselves how they could do all this fun stuff?

The simple answer was they did not have kids. When my husband and I are frustrated with our kids, we text each other pictures of Hawaii. This little moment of having someone know where I am emotionally makes a difference. For me, it means he gets it, gets me, makes me feel seen, makes me feel heard, and most of the time makes me smile.

So, find your people. Parents who meet at the playground for the first time don't admit that they were up all night. You don't tell the new friend at work that you secretly could not wait to come back to work, that maternity leave was good and all, but so is work. You don't tell strangers that you cried the two weeks before coming back to work or that at lunch you go to your car and cry about being at work. No. You tell your people.

One of the greatest gifts of my different friend groups is that some of us were stay-at-home moms, some of us were working moms, some of the working moms became stay-at-home moms, and some of the stay-at-home moms went back to work. Among us, we got to see and understand one another's struggles fully.

True, deep friendships have helped me and will continue to help me be a better parent. I love having friends now that have young children. I love to hear the stories of being a young mom. I will forever miss rocking and reading to my children at bedtime. My mom would show up after a long day at work to our house for the sole purpose of reading to her grandkids. I did not fully get it then. I do now. There is something special and holy about these moments. I also love having friends in my life who have adult children.

My friends are important to me. They allow me to be a mess. They tell me when I need to call my counselor. They let me say things that I know will stay between us. They love me entirely, and some days, I need to text someone a picture of Hawaii and smile and feel understood.

Developing a Community

We were not created to do life alone. But, at times, parenting can be one of the loneliest places. That feeling of being in a crowded room but nobody sees you? Parenting can be like that. So, how do you create this kind of community?

I have found friendships at work, church, baseball practice, soccer practice, the band booster club, the football stands, and many other places. Connecting with others can be done in so many different places. I will admit that most friendships that I created in random spaces were not deep, but they were exactly what I needed at that time. Some of the friends that I have picked up in my adult life have become my people.

Parents need community. But children need community too. One of the most important tasks as a parent is intentionally developing a web of trusted adults for your children. I have been taught by many that parents should work hard to find trusted adults who will deliberately put time and effort into their children's lives. These adults are people who will pray for your kids, connect with your kids, and develop trust with your kids, so when they need to talk to an adult (someone not their parent), they have a network of support. When you develop this web of trusted adults into your children's lives, you have also extended your own support group. This has been a game changer for me. I have not executed it as much as I wanted to, but my children do have other adults in their life who can help support them, listen to them, love them, pray for them, and I need that just as much as they do.

When you are thinking about developing your community, I must mention the significance of a faith community. This is a place where people come together to learn about faith, worship and praise God, and thoroughly love one another. I have always grown up in a faith community. I don't understand how people do life without a faith community. The churches that we have been a part of my whole life have helped me be the person I am today. I can think of key people in each congregation who have taught me, loved me, and showed me what faith could look like, feel like, and sound like. That will always be a gift to me.

The different faith communities that I have been a part of have kept our family going when we needed it the most. At one point in our lives, my husband became very ill, spent some time in the hospital, including in the ICU, and then several months at home recovering and rehabbing before going back to work. At this time in our lives, I was in graduate school and working at a new church start. Well, this little church put what we lovingly referred to as "the magic cooler" on our front porch. Two or three times a week I would find delicious meals left on the porch for our family. With the meals came more: prayers, taking the kids to school for me, picking up the kids when I could not, mowing the lawn, and taking care of us in a way that I did not know people could do. They became the family we did not think we needed. As I am writing this, I recognize that many of the people who took care of us then are not a part of our daily lives now. But they will always be a part of our family.

Whatever your community, find one. Let others connect with your family and support you when you need it the most. Let them into your space, even if it is messy. They will either help you clean it up or sit with you in the mess, whatever you need at that moment.

Parenting Perspective: Dr. Kari Roan
Parent, School Administrator

The Good

I met my husband the Christmas before I turned twelve. He had just turned thirteen, and his family had recently begun visiting our church. I still remember him turning around to look at me from where he and his family sat two rows in front of us as our mothers talked. There was a semi-instant attraction between us (as much as preteens are capable of), so we did the whole youth group hangout thing throughout our adolescence. Depending on who was retelling the origin story of us (him or me), the details varied but the gist was the same. We more or less went our separate ways when we were solidly in our teens. We loosely kept in touch because our families were so connected, and then reunited during my senior year in college. He was kind, confident, funny, and always knew who I was. I mean that in many ways. As an identical twin, I was used to being relegated to "one of the twins" or "whichever one you are," but he never confused us. On a different level, Quincy seemed to have studied me so closely that he knew things about me and my personality, often before I even became aware of those same things. I still remember him not disagreeing with my mother who said, "I know she is a lot. Thank you for loving her anyway." I, ready to discount my mom, looked at Quincy who was stifling laughter and then just hugged me as he saw the slow realization flood my face: Ohhhhhh! I am a lot? My friends who know me well also know this to be true. It is part of my charm, but it is also a very intense energy. Quincy saw that fire in me and fanned the flame higher rather than try to squelch it.

A talented musician, he proposed on a palindrome (02-02-02) with a song he wrote and recorded just for that moment in the Starbucks where we had our first date. Our wedding was everything I hoped for, and our marriage was great (not perfect, but it was great). We were friends, and we enjoyed learning about the world and each other together.

The Bad
Twelve years, two kids, one miscarriage, and plenty of

hospital visits (I had a bowel obstruction two weeks to the day before our wedding, I had a D&C for our lost pregnancy, and I had both of our children in a hospital) into our marriage, Quincy began complaining of back pain. In true marital fashion, I told him he was fine and probably just needed to be more hydrated.

Quincy's back pain intensified, and through a long series of doctors' visits that morphed into hospital stays, we learned that he had very aggressive, very advanced colon cancer . . . at age 36. Our children were six and eight upon this diagnosis. I was working full-time and was in graduate school. When the doctors tell you bad news (which you inevitably have to wait for over a weekend when none of them seem to be around), it isn't like it is in the movies. I don't think film can ever capture the enormity of those moments.

Beginning in July of that summer, when this journey started, I tried to make a meaningful connection with my kids (a hug, a funny story, something), but I am not sure how well I did. When I was not at work, I was at the hospital sitting with Quincy. He was so sick that he could not get up to go to the bathroom, so there was a portable urinal that I used to help him whenever he needed to relieve himself. He moaned in his sleep and wasn't aware of it. Between him asking for help to pee and groaning, I didn't get much sleep, and I have no idea how my kids remember that time. I am grateful to my mother and Quincy's dad for trying to make things as normal as possible for the kids by taking them to school and making sure they were fed.

The Ugly

Six months after diagnosis, God called Quincy home. I think Quincy held on so that he could celebrate one last birthday and holiday season with us. I was thirty-six and the kids had each just celebrated a birthday. About eight days after my birthday, he went back into the hospital and never came back out.

No one can prepare you for how to say goodbye to your spouse. No one can prepare you for how to help your kids say goodbye to a dad who has been good, kind, and present. I wasn't sure if I should have the kids see their dad one last time before the funeral (they had already told us there was nothing else they could do and that he would not make it past the weekend), but the hospice nurse advised that I ask the kids. I typed up what I would say to them. It was something like: Dad is going to see Jesus. Do you want to come see him before that happens? I wasn't expecting them to say yes. I recorded (not sure why—it unnerves me every time I listen to it, which has only been once) them holding Quincy's hand, him grunting and squeezing because he had lost his ability to speak but knew they were there, my son saying "Look, he's sleeping," my daughter saying, "Wait! I don't want him to go see Jesus!"

This past Father's Day, I asked them if they wanted to go to his grave to "see" their dad. Again, I wasn't expecting them to say yes. I swore silently under my breath and mustered the courage to go. We all thought it would be a good idea to bring something that reminded us of him to the cemetery. My son brought the hole-ridden blanket that used to be his dad's when he was a teenager that he now sleeps with nightly. My daughter brought the bear made out of her dad's old clothes. Seeing them stand there, him almost six feet tall and her the shape of a woman, with those childlike objects looking at their father's grave took my breath away. It was misty that day, just like it was the day we buried him. I like to think God was shedding tears at the moment.

Everything Else

I never wanted to be a single parent, but this is the lot I have been dealt. It has not been easy, but I have learned some things along the way that have been life-giving:

- I have learned that as parents we are wholly un-prepared for the totality of experiences that come with parenthood.
- I have learned that Christ gives us hope in ways we cannot fathom.
- I have learned that God places the lonely in families of choice and that he does this for our children.
- I have learned that the promise of Psalm 37:25 is true.
- I have learned that we cannot shield our children from pain, from grief, or from sadness.
- I have learned that you can do all of the "right" things, and that this will not keep pain at bay; I've learned the importance of sharing this lesson with my kids.

- I have learned that our children appreciate our honesty in the face of adversity, that they learn how to grow their emotional intelligence when we turn toward what is difficult for us and voice that it is hard.
- I have learned that God is kind even when what happens around us is cruel.
- I have learned that Jesus can take it when we say, "You have to fix this. You have to care for their hearts since you allowed this." And it will be done.
- I have learned that there are far greater things to stress about than whether we feed our kids pizza five nights a week and allow them to drink soda for breakfast.
- I have learned that we have to talk honestly with our kids about how they prefer to grieve or feel sadness, in private, with a companion, or some other way.
- I have learned that God does, in fact, provide for widows in a unique way, even when it feels like the global church falls short in that regard.
- I have learned that therapy is not a luxury but a necessity.

Holy God,

being a parent is a blessing.
It is an incredible experience filled with moments of joy,
and it can be exhausting and overwhelming at times.

I humbly proclaim that I cannot do it all on my own.
You created us for community with one another.

Open my eyes to those who are or could be a part
of my village:
Those who speak love and life into me and my family
and pray for us.
Those who surround us and stand in the gaps
where I fall short.
Those who lend a hand and offer to help
when I'm tired and in need of a break.
Help me to embrace the idea that two are truly better
than one.
May I lean on those around me and seek out their wisdom.
And, grant that I may have the courage to be vulnerable and real
with them in the ups and downs of life.

I thank you that I do not have to go on this journey alone, for you are
always with me.
And, I am grateful for those you send to walk alongside me, support
me, and remind me of your amazing love. Amen.

Rev. Pavielle Jenkins